WHEN YOU
RISE UP

WHEN YOU RISE UP

A Covenantal

Approach to

HOMESCHOOLING

R.C. SPROUL JR.

PUBLISHING
P.O. BOX 817 • PHILLIPSBURG • NEW JERSEY 08865-0817

Unless otherwise indicated, Scripture quotations are from The Holy Bible, New King James Version. Copyright © 1979, 1980, 1982, Thomas Nelson, Inc.

Scripture quotations marked (ESV) are from The Holy Bible, English Standard Version, copyright © 2001 by Crossway Bibles, a division of Good News Publishers. Used by permission. All rights reserved.

Page design by Lakeside Design Plus
Typesetting by Michelle Feaster

Printed in the United States of America

Library of Congress Cataloging-in-Publication Data

Sproul, R. C. (Robert Craig), 1965–
    When you rise up : a covenantal approach to homeschooling /
R. C. Sproul, Jr.
      p. cm.
    ISBN 0-87552-711-6 (pbk.)
     1. Home schooling—United States. 2. Covenant theology.
   3. Religious education—Home training—United States. I. Title.

LC40.S55 2004
371.04'2—dc22
2004049272

To Mark and Monique Dewey,
and the blessed blessings
He has given you.

CONTENTS

ACKNOWLEDGMENTS

If there is one lesson of history we need to learn better, it is gratitude. Because we live in an egalitarian age, we look to our fathers as if they were somehow beneath us, even as we stand on their shoulders. Like most homeschoolers, I didn't discover this notion of education on my own. Instead I learned from brave pioneers who went before me. My friend Mike Beates, the first homeschooling dad I knew, influenced me greatly. His children are a credit to his wisdom. Others who helped point the way are Gregg Harris, Michael Farris, and Raymond Moore.

The second generation has its heroes as well. I am privileged to count among my friends James McDonald at *Homeschooling Today* magazine, Phil Lancaster at *Patriarch* magazine, and Douglas Phillips of Vision Forum. Each not only has encouraged countless families back to a biblical approach to schooling, but has likewise encouraged me in sundry ways.

I would also like to thank my friends at P&R Publishing, especially Allan Fisher.

Finally, thanks are due to my dear wife Denise, my co-laborer, a help meet for me.

THE GOAL OF EDUCATION

1

War has become the dominant motif of our age. It seems that everywhere we turn there is this battle, that conflict, the other struggle. We are in the midst of a culture war, as left and right clash to define the broader culture. The federal government has declared war on terrorism, an elusive and difficult-to-define enemy. We are in the midst of an ongoing war on drugs, and before that, though Jesus told us the poor would always be with us, the federal government declared war on poverty. Even in the evangelical church, we have the worship wars—churches and denominations heatedly arguing over something indeed worthy of an argument, how to worship God.

Wars are never fought in a posture of indifference. Apathy is not something that inspires soldiers, not something you get a ration of on the front line. Wars are not often waged

11

with cool detachment. When the warfare is more rhetorical than martial, however, we especially need clear thinking. There is one ongoing battle in the culture where cooler heads rarely prevail, and for good reason. We fight the culture war, the war on terrorism, the war on drugs, the war on poverty, the worship wars in large part for the sake of our children. We want them to live in a safe world, a clean world, a world wherein they can worship God aright. But no battle touches more immediately upon our children than the education wars. Here, perhaps more than in any other battles, our hearts are on the line and our passions run deep. So coming to the education issue with clear minds is particularly important.

The education battles are myriad: battles between this federal education bill and that one, battles between this method of teaching in government-run schools and that method. We have Principle Approach Christian schools, classical Christian schools, and Christian schools that are so far behind the times that all they are is Christian schools—which shall we choose? Within the homeschool movement there are similar internal battles. Parents used to the textbooks they had as children want curriculum A, while others want curriculum C to ensure that their children have well-trained minds. And we haven't even gotten to the wars between the three groups: the government-school people hating the homeschoolers and the Christian schoolers, who of course return the favor, and the Christian schoolers and government schoolers allying themselves against those fools who won't do school.

There are at least three major battlefields in this one great war, three theaters in which the fighting goes on. We fight over who is called to do the teaching. Is the education of children a function of the state, the church, or the family? We fight over what should be taught, the content of our curriculum. Should we be reading the Bible only, the Bible plus Homer, or should we be watching television and reading *Heather Has Two Mommies*? Finally, there is the method battle. Whole language or phonics? Classical or Montessori? School-in-a-box or Charlotte Mason? These are all important questions. But before we can even try to agree on the answers, we need to see if there is anything prior we can agree on. There are three prior questions that we usually skip right over, which helps explain why we have such disagreement.

The first question is, "Is education important and valuable?" Here we have universal agreement. At the century's turn, as a nation we were spending $754 billion a year on education, including both voluntary expenditures and tax money.[1] That's more than three-quarters of a trillion dollars. To make sure you grasp the enormity of that number, let's see it in its fullness: $754,000,000,000. That number ought to suffice to answer our first question. Everybody agrees that education is important.

The second question is, "By what standard?" The source for our answers as to how Johnny should be educated is not John Dewey or Thomas Mann. Nor is it the National Educa-

---

1. *Mini Digest of Education Statistics, 2002* (Washington, D.C.: U.S. Department of Education National Center for Education Statistics, 2003), 48.

tional Association or the U. S. Department of Education (even when there is a Republican in the White House). Neither do we draw our standard from John Calvin or R. L. Dabney or Dorothy Sayers. As Christians we already know the answer to the question. However much God might have gifted any education theorists through the ages, he made none of them inerrant or smarter than himself. At least those combatants in the education wars who claim the name of Christ can all agree that whatever the Bible says, that is what we must believe.

The third question relates to the first two. "Just what exactly is the goal of education?" When Alice was walking through Wonderland, she found herself at a crossroads. She was confused over which way she should go. Startled by the Cheshire Cat up in a nearby tree, Alice asked the Cat which way she should go. "That depends a good deal on where you want to get to," said the Cat. Alice replied, "I don't much care where—" The Cat saucily answered, "Then it doesn't matter which way you go." How can you judge the failure or success of the $754 billion, unless you have some goal?

I once spoke at a conference on welfare reform. I was asked to address the group twice. In my first lecture, "The Abysmal Failure of the Welfare State," I argued that welfare has done nothing to help those in need—in fact, it has harmed the very people it purported to help, creating a dependency on the state. In my second lecture, "The Astounding Success of the Welfare State," I argued that creating a dependency on the state was the true goal of those politicians who pushed welfare programs. Success or failure depends upon the goal.

So what are we spending that $754 billion for? If you asked the average man in the street, he would probably tell you that the purpose of education is to prepare children to get good jobs when they are grown. Some might add that education exists to help children learn to get along with each other. We bus children halfway across town because the end goal is an appreciation for diversity. We skew our admissions standards for the same reasons. What if, instead of asking the man on the street, you were to quiz the religious right? Why do they want to "take back our schools"? For essentially the same reasons. That is, the religious right want children to have good jobs and to embrace their moral vision. To put it another way, we have education wars because the Republicans want to raise little Republicans and the Democrats want to raise little Democrats. Meanwhile, both claim to be simply neutral. Yet both are inadvertently bumping into a hard reality: all education is inherently religious. Robert Louis Dabney rightly argued:

> True education is, in one sense, a spiritual process. It is the nurture of the soul. Education is the nurture of a spirit that is rational and moral, in which conscience is the regulative and imperative faculty. The proper purpose of conscience, even in this world, is moral.
>
> But God is the only Lord of the conscience; this soul is his miniature likeness. His will is the source of its obligations. Likeness to him is its perfection, and religion is the science of the soul's relations to God. Let these statements be placed together, and the theo-

logical and educational processes appear so related that they cannot be separated.

It is for this reason that the common sense of mankind has always invoked the guidance of the minister of religion in the education of youth. . . . Every line of true knowledge must find its completeness as it converges on God, just as every beam of daylight leads the eye to the sun.[2]

Puritan poet John Milton understood well not only that education cannot be "neutral," but also what its purpose is: "The end of learning is to repair the ruin of our first parents by regaining to know God aright, and out of that knowledge, to love Him, to imitate Him, to be like Him."[3] How might the left howl if those on the religious right actually followed Milton's lead? Understand also that when Milton said "God," he did not mean the generic "to whom it may concern" god of our culture. He meant the God of the Bible. Instead the religious right is content to fight for cultural conservativism. Not long ago there was a public hullabaloo over an American history textbook approved by the New York State Board of Regents. It seems this text informed the students about the person and work of George Washington Carver, yet managed

2. R. L. Dabney, *On Secular Education,* ed. Douglas Wilson (Moscow, Idaho: Canon Press, 1996), 16–17.

3. John Milton, *Areopagitica* and *Of Education* (Northbrook, Ill.: AHM Publishing, 1951), 59.

to cover American history with no mention of George Washington. As bad as that is, I am puzzled that those Christians who are a part of the religious right are more upset about the absence of the father of this country than they are about the absence of the King of the Universe, the Lord of all things.

The goal of education, biblically speaking, is the goal of everything. The biblical bottom line is easy enough to find. We simply have to look to the beginning, to go back before the ruins even needed to be repaired. It is not enough to go back to the days of Ozzie and Harriet. They are the ones who brought us where we are. Instead we have to go back to the garden. In the garden God commanded Adam and Eve to be fruitful and multiply, to rule over the animals, to dress and keep the garden. They were to reflect the glory of their maker by "gardenizing" the rest of the creation, to rule under God. This is our goal—raising God-glorifying children, rather than raising responsible citizens who can manage to get along with the world around them. Consider what the psalmist wrote:

Give ear, O my people, to my law;
Incline your ears to the words of my mouth.
I will open my mouth in a parable;
I will utter dark sayings of old,
Which we have heard and known,
And our fathers have told us.

We will not hide them from their children,
Telling to the generation to come the praises of the LORD,

And His strength and His wonderful works that He
has done.

For He established a testimony in Jacob,
And appointed a law in Israel,
Which He commanded our fathers,
That they should make them known to their children;
That the generation to come might know them,
The children who would be born,
That they may arise and declare them to their children,
That they may set their hope in God,
And not forget the works of God,
But keep His commandments;
And may not be like their fathers,
A stubborn and rebellious generation,
A generation that did not set its heart aright,
And whose spirit was not faithful to God. (Ps. 78:1–8)

What might happen, if this were our model for education rather than the model put forth by the state? Too often
we who serve Christ keep the world's goal, but use a different
building. Or we keep the goal, but hire a different faculty.
Those things matter, as we will see in coming chapters. But
nothing matters more than determining where we are going.

Forget about education for a moment and try this little
experiment. Suppose you are reasonably sanctified. And suppose that God appears to you as he did to Solomon before
you. God says, "I want to give you a gift. I want to show forth

my grace by granting you your heart's desire. But instead of giving the gift to you, I'm going to give it to your children." Think for a moment about what you would ask for. You wouldn't want to be rash, so consider your answer carefully. What do you want for them? What would be your request? Would you not reply, "O gracious Lord, this is my request, that my children would dwell in your house forever. Make them yours; redeem their souls; remake them into the image of your own dear Son." If such is not your wish, shouldn't it be?

We need to think through what we value, and how much. Most mornings I exercise using a videotape that features walking. Aerobic dancing is rather too complicated for my pair of left feet. I walk three miles, and every half mile along the way I am reminded of how far I have gone. I have memorized those places on the tape. I know simply by the sound of the background music when the woman on the tape will tell me I've crossed another marker along the way. However, at the end, just when I should be so pleased to be done, she says something that grates on my soul. She asks her audience, "Should I give you the best news in the world? You've done three miles." It is a good thing to walk three miles, but not the greatest news in the world.

Consider the wisdom of John. Though he was probably not speaking of his biological children, he says, "I have no greater joy than to hear that my children walk in truth" (3 John 4). He is abundantly clear here. He doesn't say, "The best news in the world is I've walked three miles. The great news is I just saved a bundle on my car insurance. And I'm reasonably pleased to report that my children walk in the truth."

But if our great goal is to see our children embrace the gospel, what do we do once that has happened? If our child reports to us, "Daddy, while I was away at camp I threw my pinecone into the fire and invited Jesus into my heart," does Daddy in turn reply, "I can die happy now; that's all I need to know. I'm taking a nap now. Your mom and I are going to get in the RV and you'll never see us again. We're just going to run out the clock. Our work is through here." Our goal for our lives includes not only doing the work he has given us to do, what we call the dominion mandate, not only exercising dominion over our children (that is, raising them in the nurture and admonition of the Lord), but seeing that they are about the business of doing the same. You want to see your children, now abiding in the true vine, bear forth much fruit. You want them to grow in grace, to become more sanctified, to become more and more like Jesus. You want them to be consumed with pursuing first the kingdom of God.

First, we want our children to embrace the work of Christ. Second, we want them to do the work of Christ, to pursue his kingdom. And we haven't even gotten to learning to play nicely with others, or learning the periodic table. By now many of you are thinking: "I thought I was reading a book on education. This sounds more like Sunday school or youth-group material. When is this guy going to get to education?" Or: "If I tell anyone this, they'll be sure to think, 'When are we going to stop talking about Sunday school and youth group

and start talking about education?'" This is simply more evidence of our fundamental confusion over education. Thinking that education is something different from discipling our
children is a sure sign that we have been "educated" by the
state. Education is discipleship.

Not only do we have a war between those who prefer the
state or the church or the family as the locus of education, not
only do we have a war over which curriculum to use, but we
also disagree about the goal. Even within the homeschooling
movement, there is a battle between those who are for academic excellence and those who are for moral excellence. What
is confusing in this battle is that academic excellence and
moral excellence are not necessarily at odds. Both sides recognize this, and before the battle begins, both sides insist with
vigor that they are for both academic and moral excellence.
Yet there is a real battle. How do we resolve this?

The truth is that both sides are saying, "Both academic
and moral excellence, but . . ." And I am no different. We are
not in favor of moral excellence because it makes you a more
diligent student. Instead we are for academic excellence because we believe such is the fruit of character. To make it even
clearer, consider this choice. Would you rather have your child
graduate at the top of his class at Harvard, become a Rhodes
Scholar, win the Nobel Prize, and serve on the board of the
Council for Secular Humanists? Or would you rather have
your child be unable to make it through the local high school,
become a garbageman, and be a godly husband and father? I
know, everyone wants both. We want our children to be godly

21

geniuses. But if we had to choose, and praise God we don't, there really is no choice.

When God regenerates a heart, that heart bears spiritual fruit. And a vital part of that fruit is a renewed mind, the capacity to look at the world through God's eyes, to see all that we do in light of serving his kingdom. When, for instance, we teach our children physics, what is the end goal? Are we motivated to do so simply because studies show that those who master physics make, over the course of a lifetime, 33 percent more income than those who don't learn physics? Is it so our children can become structural engineers and make a grand living putting up skyscrapers? Is it so in old age we can brag to the neighbors about our children's work? Or is it instead because in building such buildings our children exercise dominion, turn dirt into shelter, and in so doing serve others?

Suppose also that we are focused on issues of the heart, that we are seeking to cultivate the fruit of the Spirit in our children. Even here we can take a wrong turn. What motivates us? The fruit of the Spirit doesn't exist so that our children can become heirs of Dale Carnegie, be hugely popular, or become prom queen or class treasurer. Rather, we teach our children these things so that they might, in obedience to God, live in peace with all men, as much as is possible. In short, as we make all our decisions and work them out, we must think through how our thoughts and actions relate to the commands of God. We need to excise from our thinking the merely normal or conventional. All we do for our children must be about raising them in the nurture and admonition of the Lord.

Satan's pull is strong. We are all in the grip of an ideological and a practical inertia. We are prone to slip back into how we've always done things, unless we remain vigilant. In a coming chapter I will emphasize the Bible's importance not in but as our curriculum. It is an emphasis I bring every time I speak on the subject of education. And every time I find myself having an internal tug-of-war. On one shoulder I have a devil whispering in my ear. On the other side I have an angel. The question is (and I can't tell you which side is the devil and which the angel, or there would be no more tug-of-war), "Should I throw them a bone, or should I not throw them a bone?" When I am emphasizing the Bible, the Bible, the Bible, I see the terror rising in their eyes. If homeschooling is a radical departure from what we're used to educationally, how much more frightening is it to throw away the mountain of curriculum we've purchased, and sit down with a Bible?

But my fear works in the opposite direction. Why should I have this tension? Why, when I believe it is utterly appropriate to teach math and physics, when I believe that both can help us better understand God, and better obey his command to exercise dominion, would I have a reluctance to concede such? Math teaches us the order of God's universe. It manifests his glory, his beauty. It is likewise a part of being a good steward. When Jesus calls us to "consider the cost," we'd better be able to calculate the costs. But I know the temptation. As soon as I concede that math is perfectly legitimate, we'll fall right back into our old pattern, seeing the Bible as a sourcebook for stuff to sprinkle over the world's curriculum. The world has determined a curriculum, and we feel tremendous pressure to follow it, if only because it is normal. And because we are Christians, we want to do normal in a Christian way. Before we can even begin to consider math, we have to start with the Bible.

How then might we do math in our homeschools, in a way that is consistent with Psalm 78, in a way consistent with John Milton's wisdom on the purpose of education, in a way consistent with the injunction in Deuteronomy 6 to teach our children when they lie down and when they rise up? Is it sufficient to stop and say a prayer or two before getting down to brass tacks? It's perfectly appropriate to pray before we do our math. I'm certainly not against prayer. But how you teach math rightly is by always remembering why you teach math, and more important, by always reminding the children. We must first confess, then profess that two and two make four—not apart from Jesus, not beside Jesus, but because it is Jesus' two and Jesus' two and Jesus' four. It all belongs to him. We confess and we profess that he invented math and he rules over it. He is the reason for it. Math is always objective, never neutral. That is, it speaks truth because Jesus is the truth.

Let's look again at the psalm, and note first the beauty of it. This, remember, is not a mere lesson to be taught. Instead it is a song and a prayer of God's people. Asaph begins by encouraging the people to listen:

Give ear, O my people, to my law;
Incline your ears to the words of my mouth.

I will open my mouth in a parable;
I will utter dark sayings of old,
Which we have heard and known,
And our fathers have told us. (Ps. 78:1–3)

Covenant theology wasn't invented at the Reformation. The notion of familial solidarity before God that is so central to the homeschool movement is trumpeted here in this psalm. What Asaph is saying is as simple as it is beautiful: "I'm going to tell you what my father told me, and his father told him, and his father told him, and his father before him told him to tell him." The promise is that he will tell God's wisdom, God's words, that have been passed down from one generation to the next. There is nothing new under this sun. Asaph doesn't draw the people's attention by promising to bring the latest research, the latest folly from the enemies of God.

Asaph's message not only passes down from one generation to the next, but is itself the message that must be passed down from one generation to the next. That is, Asaph isn't just telling multigenerational secrets, but the secret itself is, "Pass it on to the next generation." This is always a critical part of God's covenant. To simply fulfill the immediate demands of the law is never enough. It wasn't enough that Abraham should receive the mark of the covenant. Nor was it sufficient that he should place that mark on Isaac. Rather, Abraham was commanded to teach Isaac to teach his own sons the covenants of God. In simplest form, the covenant God has made with man is simply this: Love, trust, and obey God . . . and teach your children to do the same. And to take it one step further, we haven't taught our children to do the same unless or until we have taught them to teach their children.

Like Asaph, I try to teach my own children this same thing during family worship. (Family worship is neither a class in our homeschool nor set apart from our homeschool, but is rather part of the warp and woof of our family life, both life and school—more on that in a later chapter.) When I preach to the children, having read a portion of the Bible (my sermons during family worship generally last from thirty to forty-five . . . seconds), I remind them that it is not enough that they should know what the Bible is teaching. They must teach their own children these same truths. In like manner, if I fail to teach my children to teach their children, I have failed to keep covenant.

I'm convinced that failure to understand this multigenerational call of the Christian family is at the root of our failure to manifest the kingdom of God, that this is why we seem always to take two steps forward and one step back. We haven't taught enough levels of this. We must with sincerity and zeal teach our children to teach their children to teach their children to teach their children to teach their children . . . to keep going until the King's return. Instead we produce the children of Ephraim, children who do not know who they are or whose they are.

Our vision for our homeschool, for the raising of our children in the nurture and admonition of the Lord, is not something we do just because we're supposed to. Rather, it is our very vision for making manifest the kingdom of God. And that vision of the kingdom of God isn't something only for today or off at a great distance. It is this generation's changing, through the Holy Spirit's power, the hearts of the next generation, and then their changing the next generation, and the next and the next. It is generation after generation after generation of building the kingdom, growing to be more like Christ, to love him, to imitate him, to know him aright.

Perhaps even before we ask, "What is education for?" we should ask a prior question, "What are children for?" The Westminster Catechism teaches us that man's chief end is to glorify God and enjoy him forever. Of course, the Westminster Assembly met long before the advent of political correctness. When they spoke of "man's" end, they weren't suggesting that women were to serve some other goal. "Man," in this context (as in this book as well), refers not only to males but also to females. But it is broader still. "Man" covers not only the gamut of genders, but the gamut of ages. In short, children's chief end is to glorify God and enjoy him forever.

This summary of man's end brings together the Bible's varying language on the same theme. That is, we are given several "bottom line" assessments of our calling. God begins with the dominion mandate, to exercise dominion over the creation. And since God doesn't change, that ultimate goal abides. The goal is restated in Ecclesiastes—the sum of the matter is this: to fear God and obey whatsoever he commands (Eccl. 12:13). And then Jesus reiterates the same theme in a slightly different key when he tells us that we ought to seek first the kingdom of God, and his righteousness. Our children are made to seek God, as are we. Therefore, if we are to train our children rightly, we must expunge from our own hearts that overarching agenda of the culture around us, the pursuit of personal peace and affluence.

So I am sometimes troubled by how we homeschoolers measure our success. It seems that every few months the headlines tell us of another triumph, that this homeschooler got a perfect score on the SATs or the other won the national spelling bee, or a third the Young Inventors contest. And we present this as evidence that we are doing a good thing in homeschooling. Of course, there is nothing wrong with homeschoolers' achieving, nor is there anything particularly surprising about it. But these are not our successes.

Our headlines, instead, should be about stories such as this. Several years ago I took three of my children to the grocery store: Campbell, then six, Shannon, four, and Delaney, three. Not only do I have a pattern of taking our children with me, but we also have a pattern for how we go through the store. We begin with fruits and vegetables, and then finish at the bakery section. At our local store, the good folks behind the bakery counter give away cookies to little children. This too is a part of our pattern. Delaney, with a year's experience of going shopping with Daddy, hadn't quite learned all the habits. So every week she had to ask, "Can we get a cookie, Daddy?" She worries unduly, because her daddy is so cheap that it doesn't matter if we have stopped at the grocery on the way home from a tour of the candy factory. The cookies are free, so the answer is always "Yes."

The lady behind the counter gave Campbell his cookie and Delaney hers. I did not get one for Shannon, for though she likes cookies, she isn't yet adept at eating them. (My daughter Shannon is mentally retarded, with the mental ability of an 18-month-old.) I realized at this point that I had forgotten piecrusts for my wife (who is probably socking me in the arm right now for letting you know she doesn't make her own crusts—though she does make our bread, oatmeal, granola, etc.), so I left the children and the buggy to fetch some. As I headed back, I caught my son. He did not know I was watching. As far as he knew, no one was watching him. But I saw him do it. He broke off a piece of his cookie and fed it to his little sister Shannon. He didn't do this so I would one day write about him. He didn't do this because Shannon would praise him. He did not do it for the applause of men. He did it because God has worked in his heart, because his mother is an outstanding homeschooling mom, teaching him well. That is the heart of the matter; that is what we ought to be celebrating.

I'm not arguing that it's a bad thing for children to be smart. Rather, I am suggesting that the issue of education is always the heart. Changed hearts is the goal, the function, the very purpose of education. Our goal is not multigenerational personal peace and affluence. Neither are we simply trying to raise clean-cut children. Homeschoolers are adept at doing that. And there certainly may be a parallel between being nice, and having the gentle and quiet spirit the Bible calls us to. But what we want is the changed heart.

What is your goal? What are you shooting for? Even if you answer, "Building the kingdom of God," you might still have it wrong. Be careful here. We are not training our children so one day they might build the kingdom. We must remember, as we continue to grow in grace and become more effective in our calling, to ditch this notion that school is something you do for a time, and then you work. We continue to learn, while we work. And our children continue to work, while they learn. Your children are not simply in training, but are even now about the business of building the kingdom of God. What is the kingdom of God? It is that place where the least of these, Jesus' brethren, my daughter Shannon, gets a piece of cookie, because it was given to her.

As you continue to read, my hope is that our reformation is not just in our thinking. I pray we will not conclude, "Well, that was valuable and important, even interesting," then go back to the status quo. If the heart is the heart of the matter, if our children not only are learning to be kingdom builders, but are also being kingdom builders now, if we are to train our children to train their children, then this is something we need to remind ourselves of daily. The devil, you understand, is craftier than the beasts of the field. He doesn't simply whisper in our ears, "Betray your children. Raise them in the nurture and admonition of the state." Instead he distracts us, pulls us off target, makes us forget our calling, piece by piece.

Our calling is to keep our eyes on the prize—not to long to be at ease in Babylon, but to long for the city whose builder and maker is God. <u>We will not get education right until we get life right.</u> Just as so many peasants of the thirteenth century sacrificed to build the great cathedrals of Europe (which they would not see finished in their own lives), so we must look to the future, seeing the fulfillment of the promise, the consummation of the kingdom. Praise God that in his grace we get a taste each week, as we enter the worship experience in our weekly rest, of our eternal rest.

May we remember as parents that we are his children, and that he is about the business of changing our hearts, of repairing our ruins, of remaking us. And though he has not finished with us, he has placed in our care his children. May he in his grace keep our hearts aflame for these children. May he give us minds like steel traps that we would never be distracted, that we would not forsake our calling. May he, the great Steward, make us faithful stewards of children, the most precious gifts, of which is the kingdom of God.

PARENTS: GOD'S CHOSEN TEACHERS 2

Having succumbed to the temptation or having acted in wisdom to suggest that there is a place for math and for physics, we can move on. We have established that while we want smart and godly children, character is the highest goal, the very center of our educating. We have determined that we teach our children that they might know God and serve him. We agreed that if we cannot see God and his glory in the study of astrophysics, then we have no business studying it or teaching it to our children. But we can see God there because he made the physics, he made the stars, he made it all. And if we are genuinely motivated to know these things that we might know him, then we are indeed pursuing both academics and character.

It's much the same with Latin. I am my children's Latin teacher. My two oldest, Darby and Campbell, are studying what too many call a dead language. Why am I doing this? What motivates me? Am I teaching them Latin so they can read Seneca in the original, and therefore capture all the nuances of his wisdom? No, I am teaching them Latin because of the effect it has had on our language—they will understand English better if they learn Latin. Secondly, in a curious way Latin is a powerful aid to the study of logic. Latin must be decoded. Learning to decode Latin words has much in common with learning to decode arguments. But why in turn do I want my children to know logic? Because logic is a prerequisite for knowing. Without logic they can understand nothing, including the Word of God. They study Latin for language and logic, to know better who God is.

If they master Latin sufficiently to read Seneca, that's an added bonus. The benefit is not that they will find in Seneca a second source of wisdom. Rather, in reading Seneca they might learn more about God. God, after all, made the Roman Empire. God in his providence created the Roman worldview. He did all this for the express purpose of building his kingdom. In short, anytime we are studying history we are studying the providence of God, and therefore learning more about him.

It is wise for us to understand something of the State School Empire's worldview. To begin to undo the unspoken assumptions left in our own minds after receiving the state's version of education, we must have some understanding of its perspective on the issue. Consider, for a moment, this question: what are two reasons why character is not taught in state schools? (Leaving aside, of course, that a faux version of character is taught there, that the state does manage to pass along its "values" to its students.) The first reason is fairly obvious, and is at the root of the school wars in our culture. Teaching character requires a standard of behavior that is transcendent. It requires an absolute. Whose absolutes will be taught? The state, arguing from its understanding of the First Amendment, can't allow the intrusion of religion into the state sphere. But without religion there can be no character.

Why then are the schools still open? How is it, given this unsolvable dilemma (the state cannot sanction any religion and without a religion there can be no promotion of character), that the whole experiment hasn't been scrapped? In part the answer is found in the second answer to our earlier question. Schools do not teach character because, everyone seems to believe, "that's the parents' job." This vision of state education is "secular" in that it aims to teach only those things that do not touch on the transcendent. Here again the late R. L. Dabney saw his future, our present, as he considered this option over a hundred years ago:

> The only other alternative is to secularize the teaching in the public schools completely, limiting it to matters merely secular. The parents of the Church are left to supplement it with such religious teaching as they may please, or none. Some Christians, driven by the difficulty which public schools create, adopt this conclusion. . . .
>
> It is properly the whole man or person that is educated, but the main subject of the work is the spirit.

Education is the nurture and development of the whole man for his proper end. That end must be conceived rightly in order to understand the process, and even man's earthly end is predominantly moral.

If dexterity in any art, as in the handling of printer's type, a musket, or a power-loom, were education, its secularization might be both possible and proper. . . . "Why may not the State teach reading and writing without any religious bias? Why not do it as a mechanic teaches his apprentices filing, planing, hammering?" Because dexterity in an art is not education.

The latter nurtures a soul, the other only drills a sense-organ or muscle; the one has a mechanical end, the other a moral purpose. This answer cannot be met by saying, "Let it then be agreed that the State is only teaching dexterity in letters."[1]

These two answers in one sense are one. The state cannot teach character because (a) it has no absolutes from which to draw, and (b) parents do have absolutes and should draw on them. If the state cannot teach absolutes, and education requires the teaching of absolutes, it follows of necessity that the state cannot educate. But people are unused to seeing education in moral terms. They are used to seeing it in terms of dexterity. The trouble is, children are children. They don't rec-

1. R. L. Dabney, *On Secular Education*, ed. Douglas Wilson (Moscow, Idaho: Canon Press, 1996), 12–13.

ognize the existence of this magic line that supposedly separates morality and dexterity.

To help people understand the inescapable nature of morality in education, I sometimes ask them how they would feel to have their children enrolled in a Nazi school system. Do we want our children being taught that it is a good thing to murder those whom the state deems undesirable, or not? This is a moral issue, and any school that even ignores it speaks moral volumes. Again we are left with the question of whose moral system we are going to use.

The answer is the same for any school, whether a state school, a church school, or a homeschool. Because all education is inherently religious, every school will always pass along the moral convictions of the sponsoring organization. You don't have to be a Christian to see this. The state passes along its moral vision, the church passes along its moral vision, and the family does the same. This notion that the state in doing education is a-moral, irreligious, is a-true, and irridiculous. The notion of neutrality is a fraud, a scam.

So we come back to the parents. Doesn't it make sense that since we can't all agree on a moral standard, parents should pass on their own convictions to their own children? Why don't we, instead of having titanic battles at the local school board meeting, live and let live? Is it because we are a nation of do-gooders? Perhaps the temptation to seize power from the state and to use it to create disciples of our vision out of other people's children is just too great. We frankly don't trust other people to educate their own children.

I sense this whenever my conversations move from an explanation of how my own family homeschools, to my conviction that every family ought to homeschool. Those with whom I have these conversations usually move from a grudging acceptance to horror. "Oh," they'll say, "you'll do fine as a homeschooler. You're articulate and well educated. You have a nice haircut, and your nails are clean. You work behind a desk. You'll do fine. But please, you can't possibly think those *other* people could do a good job, do you? We need government schools to protect children from those other people." Now, who those "other" people are can change from conversation to conversation. To a nice, moderate left-winger, those "other" people are crazed fundamentalists who think God made the world and doesn't much like state schools. Those people might teach their children some really crazy stuff. A similar pattern, though, exists among comparatively conservative Christians. My Christian friends don't worry about me homeschooling. But they do worry about those "other" people, the people on the other side of the tracks. We must have government schools because those people who live off the government certainly can't be trusted to teach their children.

So even Christians accept the premise that we need somebody we approve of to teach morals; therefore, we are going to tax everybody to do it. We end up fighting over whose money will pay to teach whose children whose morals. But if we understand that character is the center of education, it seems the issue should be settled. If the 80 percent of evangelical parents whose children are being educated by the state realize that the state is determining the absolutes (all while denying that there are absolutes), perhaps they would no longer render to Caesar the things that are God's. ⟵

I'm afraid, though, that the state schools have taught us this lesson too well, that we should not think on such things. I'm afraid it is the state's success in inculcating a worldview about education that keeps us from adopting a biblical view. The patterns that shape our thinking begin with our own education, which is why even so many homeschools are little better than schools at home. The state's goal is to create loyal servants of the state. The loyal part is fairly easy to see. But the servant part we miss. The state wants higher test scores because higher test scores mean higher wages, and higher wages mean higher taxes. Schools, in short, are not only tax consumers, but tax producers.

The second factor shaping our understanding of education is industrialism. Now, we need to be careful here not to get confused. I'm not grumbling about industry. To fault industrialism is no more a condemnation of industry than to fault humanism is to fault humans or to fault feminism is to fault that which is feminine. That *-ism,* as my father taught me, changes everything. With it we move from a concept to a worldview. Industrialism is a worldview that comes out of and has been shaped by industry, which in turn has changed our view of education. It gave us the factory model of education.

If we learned much American history, we remember the impact of Samuel Colt. He is remembered for two interrelated cultural contributions. First, he is known for making guns.

39

Second, he is known for how he made the guns. He was among the first not only to mass-manufacture a given good, but also to do so using standardized parts. He was one of the fathers of the assembly line. The assembly line has standardized parts, all of which are laid out in their appropriate places in the manufacturing process. Person A has the task of putting all the cylinders in all the guns, while person D is charged with putting on the nice pearl handles. Person G, farther down the line, puts the sights on the gun barrels. Person A doesn't perform person D's job. He's the cylinder guy, and that's what he deals with all day. Person D doesn't do person G's job either. The cylinder guy knows cylinders, the handle guy handles, and the sight guy sights.

We call this in economics the division of labor, which brings with it, to be certain, a fair amount of tedium. But it likewise does wonders for productivity. The division of labor is not a bad thing, in its place. As far back as Cain and Abel, we see something of this principle: Cain is a dirt farmer and Abel a rancher. If it weren't for the division of labor, I'm confident that this book would be falling apart in your hands. Writing books I have some experience at. Binding books, on the other hand, requires an actual skill, one that I don't possess.

The issue before us, however, is more education than economics. The government school system has adapted the notion of a division of labor, or a factory model. The school serves as the assembly line, and the students are the parts. The process, much like the manufacturing of a Colt .45, turns out a standardized product. Of course, as those products have over the past several decades proved to be standardly inferior, we hear the cry from the state and their own experts (those who are specialists at saving "our" children) that they need more time. If only we will give them our children earlier, let them keep them longer, give them more money, then they would do better.

The experts insist that since they are the experts and we are not, therefore we are not qualified for the task at hand. After the "socialization" objection, which we will deal with in a later chapter, probably the next most common objection to homeschooling is that parents simply aren't qualified to teach. The objection might come in the slightly varied form, "How do you know you'll do a good job?" Or it might come in a more specific form, such as the objections I received when my family first started homeschooling: "Oh, R. C., we know you have wide and varied interests, all within the realm of liberal arts. We don't doubt that you will do well teaching your children literature, economics, history. But come now, R. C., do you really think someone like you can teach physics?"

Here again we have to go back to the goal, to rethink our most basic assumptions. We are rather adept at confusing what might be helpful with what is necessary. This first came home to me when I lived in a big city and got the Sunday paper each week. I had a particular ritual by which I read the paper. I would rearrange the sections in order to suit my interests. The best stuff, like the comics and the sports page, I would put on the bottom of the pile. The sections that interested me least I put on top. And on top of that I would put all the circulars and fliers, the colorful parts that told us what was on sale at Wal-Mart or the local grocery store. As I flipped through these pages, I would from time to time come across an item I had never heard of or seen before. One store might have this great container for storing all your videotapes. I would think, "Wow, how did I make it through life this far, without one of these handy storage containers? Why, my collection of "The Andy Griffith Show" is just stacked here and there. What I need is the nice plastic box."

Every new thing I saw seemed eminently reasonable to me. My dear wife got excited about things she wasn't even missing the week before. Occasionally I would point this out to her: "But dear, we didn't have this last week, and you didn't say, 'We need this,' " and she would reply, "That's because I didn't know about it." We eventually agreed that looking through these circulars wasn't the healthiest thing in terms of our battle with contentment. Better to get rid of the circulars than to pluck out our eyes.

This temptation, however, is far broader than advertisements. Too often we come to the question of education and wonder how, if we homeschool, we'll ever manage to have PTA meetings and parent/teacher conferences. How will our children get to perform in a school play, or work on the yearbook, or be in a yearbook? How will they learn trigonometry, play field hockey, or go to the prom? I would suggest that among those homeschoolers who are thinking of quitting, this is the second most common motivator. (The first is rather simple: "This is hard work.") We think the kids could play in the band, play football, or do this or that at the state school. I can't provide these experiences, so maybe I should send them off. Mr. Colt, after all, made a whole lot more guns, and more reliable guns, than those who came before him. He made them cheaper, too. Maybe I should just leave this to the experts.

Once more, let's come back to the goal. This, friends, is the key of staying strong on this issue. The devil's tactic is always simple distraction. Are we trying to raise a Heisman-winning quarterback or a godly man? I have a friend who illustrates the point in a powerful, surprising way. He might be speaking to a woman who is thinking of turning back or who can't quite get the courage to start homeschooling. In her humility she knows she wasn't the best student in the world when she was in school. Her own mother questions her qualifications, as does her neighbor. Maybe this mom went to college or maybe she didn't. But she isn't overfilled with intellectual confidence. My friend patiently listens while she highlights her mental weakness. Then he makes it worse. He asks, "What are the three main forms of rocks?"

Usually the woman is doubly puzzled. First, she has no idea where the question came from. She suspects that perhaps my friend hasn't been paying attention to the conversation. And second, of course, she is puzzled because she can't for the life of her remember the correct answer. My friend will wait patiently while she tries to construct an answer. "Um, is it sedimentary, Ignatius, and moon rocks?" My friend still won't let her off the hook. "You're considering homeschooling, and you don't even know the three main forms of rocks?" As the

43

woman becomes increasingly crestfallen, he smiles and says, "Yet you manage to be a godly young woman."

Do you understand the point? Just because some administrator or school board member thinks you need to know something doesn't mean it is essential to godliness. Remember, the Word of God equips us for every good work—the periodic table won't help a bit. And, in case you're consumed with curiosity—sedimentary, igneous, and metamorphic.

If your goal is to raise children who know the different forms of rocks, you might be wise to put them in contact with someone who knows. But if your goal is to raise from godly children godly adults, then you are the one for the job. By the way, that doesn't mean your children will never know the three main forms of rocks. After all, just a few moments ago you didn't know them, and now you do, all without the help of a state school. The teacher need not always be superior to the student in whatever is taught. Every major-league baseball team employs at least one batting coach. But there isn't a single batting coach who is a superior hitter to the people he is coaching. If he were a better hitter than the players he teaches, he would be the one playing. Tiger Woods has a coach who isn't a better golfer than Tiger Woods and isn't even good enough to play on the tour. If we are going to worry about our children's ability to learn things we don't know, let's worry about things worth knowing. You want people of character teaching your children. If that's not you, it needs to become you.

If we would simply believe the Bible, we wouldn't tie ourselves into such knots. We don't have to theorize, guess, or strategize our way through these things. The experts are always telling us we have to rely on the experts. But the Expert says otherwise. We've seen this in the last generation on a different issue. Dr. Jay Adams became widely known in evangelical circles when he first published his book *Competent to Counsel*.[2] Though that book is one of the most influential books published in the Christian realm in the last forty years, too few even remember the real point. Dr. Adams was not seeking his place among psychological theorists. He wasn't trying to bring a new theory that would oust Rogers or Skinner, Jung or Freud. The central point was not to introduce nouthetic counseling to the world. Instead the point was to introduce pastors to their calling. It was to remind the church of simply this: pastors are competent to counsel. God has gifted them with what it takes to care for their people. A pastor doesn't look at his degrees to see if he is competent to counsel. Instead he looks out at the congregation to see if he is competent to counsel. If God has placed sheep there, they are his job.

There is a similar test I like to offer to determine whether or not you are competent to homeschool. You don't have to go to college to get a degree in education. (In fact, that degree might prove to be counterproductive because education programs prepare you to teach how the state wants you to teach.) You don't have to have teachers in your family background. Nor is it necessary that you were once the teacher's pet, or are

2. Jay E. Adams, *Competent to Counsel: Introduction to Nouthetic Counseling* (1970; repr., Grand Rapids: Ministry Resources Library, 1986).

an expert in clapping erasers. The test is rather simple to take. It should take only a few minutes, and then you will know. The first thing you do is wait until it is late at night. Then, very quietly, go from room to room in your house. Peek in carefully, and see if you find any sleeping children. Then be sure that these are your own children. If there are wee ones in your home during the wee hours, and if they belong to you, you are competent to homeschool. The true Expert on education is the very One who gave you these children.

In fact, there is an important danger in becoming an expert. Going back to our factory model, we see that people are trained for only one small job in state schools. They are incompetent to deal with the very variety that is real life. While there is certainly a potential danger for the generalist who studies widely, learning less and less about more and more, eventually knowing nothing about everything, the greater danger is the specialist, who narrows the scope of his learning more and more until finally he knows everything about nothing. We are more apt to run into everything as we set about the sacred task of raising godly seed.

God gives us the children he gives us, and gives us the lives he gives us, for his purposes. He prepares us today for our calling tomorrow, day by day. He does this perfectly because he is sovereign. He is the one who tells us in Deuteronomy 6, "Hear, O Israel: The LORD our God, the LORD is one! You shall love the LORD your God with all your heart, with all your soul, and with all your might. And these words which I command you today shall be in your heart; you shall teach them diligently to your children, and shall talk of them when you sit in your house, when you walk by the way, when you lie down, and when you rise up. You shall bind them as a sign on your hand, and they shall be as frontlets between your eyes. You shall write them on the doorposts of your house and on your gates" (Deut. 6:4–9). Here the Expert, the One who knows everything about everything, lays down this obligation on parents. The text, please note, doesn't say, "Make sure that this gets done. Make sure your children learn these things."

This is important not to miss. We Americans are a prag-matic people. Our concern is that a job gets done. We don't much concern ourselves with how it gets done, far less who does it. Even my children suffer from this error. When I tell child A, "Please clean up the living room," it's not unusual to hear the response, "Don't you think it would be better if child C cleaned this up? She, after all, made this mess, and it would be a good thing for her to learn." This happens often enough that I don't even have to think about my response: "I didn't ask you who you thought should clean the room. I asked *you* to clean it up." In like manner, when God commands that someone do a job, it is arrogant and disobedient to pass that job on to someone or something else. Truth be told, I'm baf-fled over why we seem to have lost sight of this. How can so many great men for so long have missed this? Martin Luther argued for the establishment of state schools in his day. Even though Luther was supporting state schools that acknowl-edged the lordship of Christ in principle (as our state schools do not), that doesn't excuse him for denying the lordship of Christ in giving to the state the charge God gave to families.

Because God made this call, our attempts to wiggle out of that responsibility avail nothing. If you stand before God at your death and he says, "Your children are the greatest Christians since John the Baptist," who gets the credit for that? God does, of course. Or suppose God says, "Your children made it into the kingdom by the skin of their teeth. Much of what they devoted themselves to on earth is wood, hay, and stubble." Or sadly, if he should inform you that your children are not within the kingdom, do you think you can escape the responsibility? Can you say to God, "Lord, do not be angry with me—it was the principal you gave me"? Or, "Lord, what could I do? I was offered that promotion, and where we went the school superintendent was particularly hostile to the faith. You gave me that opportunity. Why is it my fault that the schools were so liberal?" Eternity is on the line, and we will answer for our children.

This doesn't mean that parents are the only ones to blame. Pastors take some responsibility, not because they failed to construct quality Christian schools, but because they failed to teach their people the whole counsel of God, which includes Deuteronomy 6. (By the way, please remember that Deuteronomy 6 is not some biblical backwater. It contains the _shema_ (v. 4), the single most important verse in the Old Testament to the faithful Jew, followed by the great commandment (v. 5), followed by the command to teach the children.) The shepherd will answer when his flock fails to heed the command of God, but the local shepherd, the father, will answer for his children.

This same buck-passing, this responsibility drift, is common enough in the local church, where the notion of the expert is strong. Congregations vote to call a "youth pastor," a young man whose job is to do the job of the men who hired him. He is the one who will instruct the youth on the faith, at least when they're not busy playing foosball and eating pizza. He is the one who is called to undo the education that the state provides for them. The division of labor prevails. Daddy is too busy making money (as is Mommy most of the time) to actually train the children. So we ask the state to do it for us, and pay our taxes. Then we in turn ask the church to do the rest of the job, and pay for that with our tithes.

But while we think we're paying the youth leader or the Christian school teacher to inculcate in our children our biblical convictions, we should not be surprised to find out that this isn't on their agenda. Why do people go into Christian education or become youth pastors? It certainly isn't the money. No, they take these jobs with far more selfless motives. They take these jobs because they want to change the world, to shape the minds of those students. They not only understand that he who rocks the cradle rules the world, but they have convinced parents to pay them to rock the cradle.

This is perfectly understandable. I teach people in any number of contexts. I pray, as you read, that I am being of service to you. But the center of my calling is to raise up godly seed, to teach them what the Bible teaches. My job, in short, is to Sproulinate them, or Sproulicize them. Now, of course there are places I am wrong. But I believe everything I believe

49

because I believe the Bible teaches it. Where I am wrong, I will answer for it. You can't escape God's call on your life. But when you look at it rightly, you don't want to.

Suppose, for instance, that I'm the Mr. Chips of Christian schools. All the kids just love me. I'm so good that I become a nationwide story, appearing on television, on radio, and in magazines, as people talk about what a wonderful way I have with children. Suppose my smiling face is on the cover of *Christianity Today*. Now, suppose while all this is happening, my children reject the faith. Suppose they become covenant-breakers. Do you think I would trade my six children for the thousands I might help as Super-Teacher? Not on your life.

But my goal isn't to put pressure on parents, to warn them that if they fall down on this burden, God will get very angry. Instead we should understand that teaching our children is our delight, our joy, our opportunity. When we see spending time with them as a burden, rather than a joy, we see further evidence of how encultured we have become. Children, biblically speaking, are a blessing from God. And we ought to seek out time with blessings from God, not plot out ways to avoid them, or hand them over to others.

But we are not through yet. Not only does God command us to teach our children, not only are we blessed as we obey, but also we have already so promised. We are cornered. A few years ago a dear family friend became an ex-friend. She was excommunicated from her church for unrepentant adultery. Before the excommunication became final, I took some

50

time to write these words to her: "There are only three sacred vows we are called to make. When Jesus enjoins us to let our yea be yea and our nay be nay, he isn't saying we can never speak vows. Rather, he commands that we never enter into them frivolously or over frivolous matters. Those three vows are your church membership vows, wherein you publicly, formally, in a vow declare your allegiance to Christ and to his church. The second vow is your marriage vow, wherein you promise to love, honor, and obey in sickness and in health, in plenty and in want, till death do you part. And the third vow is the baptismal vows, wherein you promise to raise your children in the nurture and admonition of the Lord, wherein you vow to set before them an example of godliness. And you," I explained to this woman, "have broken all three." Of course God's grace is sufficient. But we are called to obedience, and are not to take that sufficient grace for granted. The point isn't so much, "Bear up under suffering," as it is "Be obedient." When we trust God in obedience, he gives the grace we so desperately need.

And then he blesses us. Please understand that I'm speaking from experience. I understand how the world, or what is "normal," shapes our thinking, and how our thoughts are conformed to the pattern of this world. As I mentioned earlier, I have done a fair amount of study on a broad range of subjects. Even in high school I was intent on developing a consistent and coherent biblical worldview. I understood my economics. I understood my theology. I studied the arts and philosophy. I was convinced that I was on the road to taking

51

every thought captive to the obedience of Christ. But my understanding of the family, of children, came straight from the world. I saw marriage and children as burdens, hindrances, distractions that might take away from my good time. Discovering that the Bible had a different view didn't cure me overnight. I still suffer from this sin in my life. But as I moved from ignorant disobedience, to knowing disobedience, to an attempt at obedience, I discovered that his grace is sufficient unto the day. As we enter into knowing obedience, God leads us into seeing the joy, feeling the joy.

I've met parents who have stopped homeschooling before. But I've never met a parent who complained, "This is misery, and I can't wait to be done." I'm sure there are people who do feel that way, though I've never met one. I suspect there are other reasons for their misery besides homeschooling. We will look at some of those reasons in future chapters. But for now, we need to remember an important truth. We are, most of us, parents. That includes weighty responsibilities. But we are also children. We need to remember that we are not only teachers, but also students. God, who commands that we call him Father, is our teacher. But unlike us, our Father is perfect in every way. He never grows weary. He never errs. He never thinks the devil's thoughts. Rather, our Father leads us in the good way. He not only leads us beside still waters, but also leads us in the paths of righteousness. He likewise empowers us to grow in grace and obedience. As we come to this duty, this obligation, this challenge from God, ask him as your Father for grace, strength, power, patience. Ask him (who when we ask for bread will not give us a stone) to turn our hearts back to our children. He delights to answer our prayers. If he will not give you the joy, you can be confident that he will give you the strength. He is, after all, our Father.

He is a gracious Father, who has adopted us into his family. He loves us as his children, perfectly. And he does indeed teach us. May he likewise stiffen our backbones and strengthen our hearts, that we might run well the race he has set before us, that we might not grow weary in doing good, that in turn we might honor him.

YOU SHALL SPEAK
OF THEM

3

There are a number of angles we can take when dealing with our problems. In fact, one could argue that three approaches involve the threefold office of Christ. Jesus, you will remember, is our prophet, our priest, and our king. When a priest sees a problem, his tendency is to deal with the problem from a posture of compassion. Priests, after all, serve as mediators between God and man. They are shepherds who are called to lay down their lives for the sheep, just as Jesus, the Great High Priest, did for his bride at Calvary.

Kings, however, don't tend to lead with compassion. Rather, their prerogative is to lead with power. For instance, when the disciples were frightened during the raging storm at sea, Jesus did not take them by the hand and promise to stand by their side until it was all over. In his own timing, he commanded the wind and the waves to be still—and his power to rule awed his disciples. That he is likewise a servant does not and cannot undo his kingly authority and majesty. He will, after all, one day judge all the world.

But Jesus is also a prophet, and sometimes deals with problems as a prophet does. There is a prophetic way to deal with problems, but before we can understand what that way is, we first must understand the role of the prophet. His job was not, first and foremost, to foretell the future. He wasn't a godly version of the carnival fortune-teller. Neither, however, was the prophet merely an itinerant preacher. He was a specialist of sorts, in a proper sense. His job was to bring the Word of God to bear on problems, almost always problems within God's covenant community. Just as the priest speaks to God on behalf of the people, so the prophet speaks to the people on behalf of God. The prophet is God's mouthpiece, his lawyer. He lets those in covenant with God know that they are not keeping covenant and have a duty to repent.

I serve as the director of the Highlands Study Center. The study center exists to help Christians live more simple, separate, and deliberate lives for the glory of God and the building of his kingdom. That's our fairly sophisticated way of describing the kind of teaching we do. Our message, whether we are talking about the family, the church, the state, or education, is some variation on this same theme: "Why aren't we where we're supposed to be? What is the center of our problem, what is our weakness, what have we failed to do? And what are we doing that we should stop doing?" Of course, given our purpose statement, we might appropriately give this answer: What's wrong with us is that we fail to be simple, separate, and deliberate. If we could just get those things right, then we would solve so many of the problems we suffer through in our families and communities.

But there is another way of describing what we do at the study center, a way that is less flowery or poetic. One could rightly say that what we do is point out to our brothers and sisters, and to ourselves, those places where the church is worldly. The problem with our families is that they are worldly. *Worldly*, interestingly, is a word we don't use too often anymore. We're so intent on reaching out to the world that we think the countless biblical injunctions against worldliness are simply closed-minded roadblocks on the way to winning the lost. Or worse, we reduce the scope of worldliness to a short list of particularly egregious sins. That our lives, we seem to reason, are spent in the pursuit of personal peace and affluence isn't worldliness. No, only adultery and drunkenness and embezzlement are worldly.

Worldliness is not that difficult to pinpoint. Another way the Bible talks about it is simply this—it is a lack of faith. Our problem as the people of God is that we don't have faith. Oh, I know in some sense we do. We have defined *faith* almost as narrowly as we have defined *worldliness*. Because all we're particularly interested in is securing a slot in heaven, we think of faith strictly in terms of our justification. Faith is trusting in the finished work of Christ on our behalf. And indeed it is. Having established this, if we are given to theological precision, we note the three elements of faith, complete with Latin terms. *Indicia* is the capacity to understand what it is we're to believe. *Assensus* is affirming our conviction that the message is true. There is, however, more. Satan, after all, not only understands that Jesus died to save sinners, much to his chagrin, but knows that it actually happened. The third element is *fiducia*, wherein we place our trust in what we affirm to be true, thus receiving forgiveness of our sins and the righteousness of Christ imputed to us.

But that is not the end. Faith simply means, most broadly, believing God. This is our fundamental problem. Sin, folly, destruction—a veritable Pandora's box opens up as I fail to believe God. This is true for all of us. Every time we sin (whether that sin is a self-conscious sin of commission, or failing to do what we are called to do out of ignorance or laziness, the sin of omission), we're saying to God, "You're not right; I'm right." And then we send him a cosmic raspberry. Every sin, in that it is a failure to believe God, calls God a liar. It is, as one wise theologian put it, cosmic treason.

Perhaps one reason we don't worry ourselves too much about faith is that we have kind of conceded faith to the Pentecostals, along with the Holy Spirit. When you go to a crusade or tent revival, what is the speaker always imploring folks to do? At these events the grand attraction is the spectacular healings. But there is a prerequisite. When the healings don't happen, the problem is simple enough: the people didn't have sufficient faith. It certainly isn't the healer's fault. He certainly believes. It certainly can't be God's fault, for that theology is built on the premise that God wants everyone to be well. So it must be the sick person's fault.

My goal here is not to create more Pentecostals. Rather, I want to suggest that this is actually healthier than what people in my tradition tend to do. I'm what they call a Calvinist. (If, by the way, you haven't yet put the book down, it's only because God ordained that you would keep reading from before the foundation of time . . . Still there? Good, everything's going according to plan.) Calvinists are known for their theological precision, for crossing our theological *t*'s and dotting our theological *i*'s. But we are not known either for our warm hearts or, sadly, for our godly lives.

We like to use those Latin terms. We even like to explain to others all about *indicia*, *assensus*, and *fiducia*. We'll sit anyone who is willing down in an armchair and explain how the difference between *assensus* and *fiducia* is like the difference between saying, "I believe that the chair will hold me" and sitting on the chair. No matter how mentally convinced you are that it can hold you, the chair won't actually hold you until you sit down in it. In like manner, it isn't enough to say, "Jesus died for sinners," but you must sit, rest in that truth. You must plead the blood you say is powerful unto salvation.

Why do I mention this? Because I'm afraid that too many of us, especially my fellow Calvinists, come to the Word of God with the wrong attitude. We affirm, properly and in order, that Scripture is the Word of God, that it is inerrant and infallible. We then affirm what it teaches about how we have peace with God, staunchly and rightly defending justification by faith alone against all false gospels. But then we are content to live in the realm of the *assensus*. We sit in our parlors looking so sophisticated as we debate the finer points of theology. We bicker about what is true, which leaves us with only two options. We either are spending our time defending what is false or spending our time defending what is true, but never entering into the *fiducia*. We would rather, in short, talk about the doctrine of the inerrancy of the Bible (a precious doctrine indeed) than talk about what that inerrant Bible actually says.

When I affirm that faith means believing God, what is it about or from God that we are supposed to believe? When poor deluded souls tell me that God told them he would destroy the city of Portland, Oregon, am I guilty of not believing God when I don't call all my Oregonian friends and tell them to flee from the wrath to come? What is my duty if a young lady should tell me that God revealed to her that we were to be wed? (This has happened to people I know.) Is faith believing what people say God has said? By no means. The place where God speaks, where we must in faith believe him, is in his Word, in the Bible.

As I suggest that our problem is that we don't have faith, we don't believe God, and we don't believe his Word, am I accusing us of a denial of the inerrancy of the Bible? No. If we were still talking about *assensus*, then yes, I would be arguing we don't believe in inerrancy. But to believe in the inerrancy of the Bible in *fiducian* terms, you must look at it as a lamp unto your feet. You must believe not just in your heart, but also in your hands that "all Scripture is given by inspiration of God, and is profitable for doctrine, for reproof, for correction, for instruction in righteousness, that the man of God may be complete, thoroughly equipped for every good work" (2 Tim. 3:16).

It may be that I'm preaching to the choir, that you don't have the kind of struggles I have. In my tradition we tend to come to this text and use it as a prooftext for inerrancy. But do we really think this was Paul's point? Was he saying to his beloved Timothy, "Listen up, I want you to get this doctrine of inerrancy straight"? Can you see how this approach removes us one step from the very Word of God itself? The point here isn't the truth quotient of the Bible, but the power quotient. The point is the value of the Bible in shaping our lives. Certainly we must have sound arguments in favor of inerrancy. Such is a good and sound thing to do. But that doesn't cause the devil to cower in a corner. He who is craftier than the beasts of the field delights to use such arguments as a distraction. If we would believe and value God, we must come to the Bible, seeing it not just as true, but as valuable, powerful. What has become of us that we are no longer bowled over by the fact that God speaks to us in his Word? This is God, the creator of all things. Even if there were no Bible (and once there was not), if someone showed you a piece of paper and said, "Written on this paper are the very words of God," wouldn't you want to see it? If you actually believed that God's words were on that paper, could anything keep you away, even a highbrow conversation on the doctrine of inerrancy? Wouldn't you want to know what it said? If in turn you believe that the

Bible is God's Word, you should want to know what God says. The Bible is valuable to us because it is God speaking. That is why it is the *Holy* Bible.

To long for new messages from God is to despise his Word. People who are given to this longing don't want to know what God *said;* they want to know what they think God *is saying*. But the Bible is not only all God's Word, but also his only verbal revelation to man. When the church adopts the therapeutic model of life, seeing sinners as people who need to be made well, rather than as people who need to repent, looking to psychologists for the answers is a denial of the Bible. Adopting Madison Avenue techniques for growing the church is much the same. Not only do we turn the gospel into something to sell, but in so doing we also reject the Bible. This is happening most among those who would be happy to affirm their belief in the inerrancy of Scripture.

Consider the story of Lazarus and the rich man. We turn this story into a parable about treating people well, or we turn it into a prooftext against the doctrine of soul sleep. But was that really what Jesus had in mind? Was that his goal in telling this story? What is the punch line?

Several years ago a friend sent me a copy of an appeal letter she had received from a mammoth parachurch organization. The envelope contained a headline that read something like, "God gives girl two weeks to spread gospel message." In the letter itself we were told of this sickly little girl who had come to embrace the gospel. Her illness drove her into cardiac arrest. She then had what we call an out-of-body experience where God told her that he was giving her two more weeks so that she could tell others about him. The fund-raiser was a double whammy. First, this anointed little girl had come into the kingdom through the parachurch ministry. Second, it was through that ministry that her message could go out, if we would happily open up our checkbooks.

I've never visited this organization's offices. I do, however, know several people who work there—good, godly people. Surely one of these folks, as this appeal was making its way through the office, would have said something like, "You know, this flies straight in the face of the story of Lazarus and the rich man." Listen to the conclusion of the story: "Then he said, 'I beg you therefore, father, that you would send him to my father's house, for I have five brothers, that he may testify to them, lest they also come into this place of torment.' Abraham said to him, 'They have Moses and the prophets; let them hear them.' And he said, 'No, father Abraham, but if one goes to them from the dead, they will repent.' But he said to him, 'If they do not hear Moses and the prophets, neither will they be persuaded though one rise from the dead'" (Luke 16: 27–31). Why then did this organization print and mail this appeal? It's fun, exciting, new.

The Bible is it. God is done. God is not sending little girls who have died. He is not speaking through the Blessed Virgin Mary at shrines around the globe. He's not speaking through the men and women with big hair that populate "Christian" television. Once we understand this it creates an urgency to look to the Word of God.

That Word tells us that it equips us for every good work. Well, what is a good work? What are we supposed to be doing? How do we redeem the time, since the days are evil? God's first command to man was that he should exercise dominion, that he should dress and keep the garden. And what is the center of the garden? An analogy like the one we considered earlier, about whether we strive for successful children or godly children, might help. Suppose that after many late nights in my garage, I invent an amazing widget. This particular widget is, in essence, a perpetual-motion machine. It provides a limitless supply of cheap, clean energy. Won't that do great things for our capacity to exercise dominion over the creation? Wouldn't this be a great leap forward? But then suppose that with all the vast riches I gain for this boon to mankind, I begin to lead a debauched lifestyle. Do you really think God would be pleased with me, that he would praise me for doing so well in advancing the progress of dominion? What is the center of our calling as dominion-exercisers, as gardeners in God's garden, but to sanctify ourselves and our family?

Let's look at it again: "All Scripture is given by inspiration of God, and is profitable for doctrine . . ." and then our tendency is to stop there. The Bible is indeed profitable for doctrine. As a Presbyterian minister of the gospel I must "subscribe" to the Westminster Confession of Faith, a summary of biblical doctrine composed by some of the greatest theological minds of the seventeenth century. They demonstrated that every doctrine affirmed in this extrabiblical document came from the Bible by, at every point, listing a series of "prooftext" biblical passages that taught the doctrine being affirmed in the Confession. The Bible is profitable for doctrine, but the passage continues. Understand that I love doctrine. I do not turn my nose up at doctrine—it is vital. But the Word of God goes on to say, "for reproof, for correction, for instruction in righteousness." The Bible is designed to make us godly men and women.

The Bible also tells us where to go for God's blessings. We start with the Book itself, which is indeed a great blessing. Then we open it and are told that children are a blessing from God. (Now, before I go any further, how many of you, besides my editor, think I've forgotten the subject of this chapter or, worse, of this book? Believe me, I will get us back on the path.) I want us to understand how we abuse the Bible. Too many of us adopt the world's notion of seeing children as a burden, as I once did. But sometimes those who see them as a blessing take this promise of God into their workshop and with their lathe fashion out of it a baseball bat, so they can whack around other folks who won't (or, worse, can't) have children. The message isn't simply, "Don't try to avoid children," but is instead a glorious promise from our Father. Neither do we resign ourselves to God's viewpoint, thinking, "Well, God says children are a blessing, and I suppose he ought to know. I'll never step into that blessing. God said it, though, so I won't try to avoid the little monsters."

If we actually believe this promise (see Ps. 127 for the promise itself), we not only will pray, "Lord bless us with many children, fill our quivers, increase our territory . . . ," but will likewise say of our children and to our children, "I'm glad you're here. You are a joy in my life. I miss you when we are apart." This is an important part of what it means to see children as a blessing. Note, however, that while this may be most true of your own children, it is true of others' children as well.

I remember not long ago seeking out a conversation with a gentleman in our church. He and his dear wife were expecting, and no doubt that coming baby was heavy on his mind. But I saw him having a conversation with somebody else's three-year-old daughter. That isn't so unusual, but I could tell by looking at him that he wasn't thinking, "I'm doing my duty; this is what's expected around here." Instead he was having a pleasant, sincere conversation, one that was still going on when I returned to see if he was free twenty minutes later. That is believing God. That is the *fiducia* of believing God that children are a blessing.

Once we are settled in this biblical truth, we will see our children as a profound opportunity to be about the business of building the kingdom of God. And how might that conviction change things? How would it change our view of education? Sadly, we are out pursuing personal peace and affluence—and that includes homeschooling families. They too choose homeschooling because of their conviction that their children will get a better education, so they can get into a better college, so they can get a higher-paying job. Everything works out fine until the prestigious school undoes all that you have taught your children. Some, however, try to combine these twin goals, attaining personal peace and affluence, and building the kingdom of God. These parents reason that we can build the kingdom of God by making our children CEOs and politicians. They seem to think that the reason we have so much corruption in high places is that we have the wrong people in there. If only we could get our children there, then everything would be dandy.

Here the problem isn't a bad goal, but a bad method. To want to exercise dominion, to build the kingdom of God, is a good desire. But God not only tells us to do this, but also tells us how to do it. The worldly approach, seizing power, is doomed to failure. If we want to build the kingdom, we must make our lives living sacrifices. Doing so rarely gets you on the cover of *Newsweek*. One important way to sacrifice our lives is by devoting them to training up our children in godliness, by taking up our cross, and teaching them to do the same. You won't win a Nobel Prize for raising godly children. All you'll win is crowns in heaven.

If we believed God, we would see that the Bible is valuable as the power of God unto salvation. And we would see as well that salvation has a broader meaning than getting people to pray the sinner's prayer and secure for themselves a spot in heaven. The Bible describes our salvation in at least three different ways. We are saved; we are being saved; and we will be saved. All of this salvation comes through the power of the Word.

We're so confused on this that some people think exercising dominion is bad because it delays the return of Christ. It is better, in this mind-set, for things to get worse and worse, so Jesus can come back. I have a friend, a fine godly man, but one given to this notion that the world must get worse. In print he argued that the reason we remain on earth after getting saved is strictly to tell others that they might be saved. He wants us to get as many people on the lifeboat as we can, before the entire world collapses in the rubble of despair and destruction.

All of these things come together as we consider the how of educating our children. We have already considered the goal of education, what it is we're trying to accomplish in the lives of the blessings God has given us. In the previous chapter we established that Deuteronomy 6 tells us that God calls parents to do this important job. But because the Word of God equips us for every good work, it also gives us God's methodology, his pedagogy for doing this job. In our day the home-schooling movement is growing by leaps and bounds. And that growth has meant a corresponding growth in the availability of homeschool materials, each with its own theories on how to homeschool. Not only do we have a plethora of theories, we even have one that is not a theory, what we call "school at home," simply following the pattern of the state schools in our own homes. Many of these competing theories claim to be Bible-based. But are they?

Let's look at this critical passage again:

Now this is the commandment, and these are the statutes and judgments which the LORD your God has commanded to teach you, that you may observe them in the land which you are crossing over to possess, that you may fear the LORD your God, to keep all His statutes and His commandments which I command you, you and your son and your grandson, all the days of your life, and that your days may be prolonged. Therefore hear, O Israel, and be careful to observe it, that it may be well with you, and that you may multiply greatly as the LORD God of your fathers has promised you—"a land flowing with milk and honey." Hear, O Israel: The LORD our God, the LORD is one! You shall love the LORD your God with all your heart, with all your soul, and with all your might. And these words which I command you today shall be in your heart; you shall teach them diligently to your children, and shall talk of them when you sit in your house, when you walk by the way, when you lie down, and when you rise up. You shall bind them as a sign on your hand, and they shall be as frontlets between your eyes. You shall write them on the doorposts of your house and on your gates. (Deut. 6:1–9)

We looked at this passage in chapter 2, as we recalled whom God calls to teach the children. This passage also gives us not the newest theory to come down the pike, but the oldest. This theory isn't Charlotte Mason or "unschooling" or the "Principle Approach" or the classical approach, though it has some things in common with all of them. What it gives us is as shocking as it is simple. Here is how God wants us to educate our children—he wants us to <u>talk to them.</u> This is the very substance of what education is. In our next chapter we will talk about content, but for now we are talking about methodology, a rather fancy word for talking to your children.

In our family we have a ritual to help us remember this. Whenever my dear wife gives birth, the baby goes through the usual routines. The baby is cleaned up, checked out, given to Mom to hold, and then eventually wrapped up like a loaf of bread and put in what we call the "bun warmer," a little heated bassinet on wheels. None of our children were born so fast that we didn't make it to the hospital. We always have time to pack, and my wife is a professional packer. She packs the still camera and the video camera, clothes for herself and the baby, a deck of cards to play with me, and a stack of birth announcements that she starts filling out as soon as the baby is born. I have only to pack one thing, and so far, out of six times, I've never forgotten it. I always bring our homeschool curriculum. When Denise holds the baby I kiss the baby, hug and kiss Denise, cry a little bit, and wait. When the baby is bundled up, I reach for the curriculum.

Our curriculum has sections in it for boys and for girls. The boy part has thus far been used only once, the girl part five times. To all of my girls I read Proverbs 31, the beautiful description of a godly wife and mother. To my son I read Proverbs 3, calling him to lean not on his own understanding, but to rely on the Word of God.

Why do I do this? I am matriculating my children into the R. C. Sproul Jr. School for Spiritual Warfare. (The name of our school, by the way, isn't motivated by self-aggrandizement. Rather, I have named the school for me as a memory aid, that I would remember that I am responsible for my children.) My children have just been through the trauma of birth, and immediately they are enrolled in school. Daddy talks to his children, his students.

"Surely," you may be thinking, "this can't be it. You're talking about religious education, R. C. What we really mean by education involves lesson plans and a bunch of other stuff." Or you may be thinking, "Great lesson, R. C., on how to do Sunday school, but this is not a lesson in education." The truth is, friends, this is it. This, God promises, is the way in which we can ensure for our children that it will go well for them in the land. This is how we raise our children to be godly men and women. Do we believe the Bible or don't we? Ask yourself for a moment how the Hebrews educated their children. This is not only how they did it, but also how we are doing it.

Not long ago I had a visitor in my house. Though he isn't a Christian, he is a comparatively upright man. He loves his wife and his children. He asked me, as I was leaving to teach on homeschooling, "R. C., what are you teaching on tonight?" I knew this man had his children enrolled in the state schools. I was in a difficult place, not wanting to offend. I explained rather vaguely that I'd be talking about Deuteronomy 6. My friend wasn't satisfied, and asked rather directly, "What's in Deuteronomy 6?" What could I say but, "Well, it talks about the calling of parents to train their children up properly." Then, with a strange mix of incredulity and admiration, he asked, "Do you really believe that what Moses wrote for those people back then is still for now?" But one need not be a nominal member of a liberal church to think in those terms. When confronted with this passage, 80 percent of evangelical parents still decide to give their children over to the state for their education. Whether they say it or not, they must conclude, "That was then, this is now. This is not for me." What a contemptuous way to treat the Word of God.

Have you ever asked yourself, HWJS—how was Jesus schooled? I'm almost embarrassed every time some homeschooler thinks it would be a powerful apologetic for the practice if we could list some of the most powerful and important homeschoolers in history. We claim Abraham Lincoln as one of ours. Thomas Edison, remember, flunked out of school, so must have been taught at home. But who was the smartest, the most influential homeschooled student in the history of the world? Jesus. If we have Jesus, why do we need Lincoln?

Remember also that Jesus' pedagogical practice, not surprisingly, followed the Old Testament model. Jesus was what is known as a "peripatetic" teacher. That simply means that he tended to walk while teaching. And how did he teach? By talking with the disciples. He walked around and he talked. His method was simple: simple conversation.

Though the plain command of Deuteronomy is sufficient to settle the matter, we can see more of God's wisdom in how Jesus taught. Teaching is by its nature relational. More is involved in teaching but it is principally a conversation between parents and their children. The conversation is not limited to the school hours of 8:00 to 3:00. Rather, the teaching is done during the entire day, every day. School is never out of session, for we converse when we lie down, when we rise up, when we walk by the way. Understand that this is Hebrew idiom. When Moses says, "When you lie down and when you rise up," the point isn't to exclude sitting or kneeling. The point is that we teach all the time.

In addition, we teach always in the context of real life. Biblical learning is <u>organic, rather than abstract.</u> Why is that? Because if you spend all your day in the abstract, there will never be any food on your table. Let's not separate shop class or home economics from school. Rather, we teach in the context of daily life precisely because children will apply what we teach in the context of daily life. In so doing we make manifest the reign of Christ. We show our children how his reign controls all things.

Remember, however, that this passage tells us not only what we are called to do, but also what we will do. Whether we like it or not, we do teach our children when they lie down and when they rise up. Psychologists put this idea in slightly different language, but make much the same point. They tell us, "<u>More is caught than taught.</u>" Whatever path you take, whether you abdicate your responsibility, or whether you delegate it, your children will still learn from you. When you send them off for seven hours a day to a place where Jesus cannot even be acknowledged, they will learn more from that than they will from their Sunday school lesson. They will learn that Jesus is for Sundays. Even when you spend the dinner hour trying to debrief your children from their day at the state school, you still tell them that the error they received isn't serious, and can be dealt with over a simple meal. They will also learn, loud and clear, that you would rather they be away than with you, even if you serve them cookies and milk when they come home and say how much you missed them.

Isn't it ironic that Satan has convinced our culture that the worst thing parents can do is to give up their children? Expectant moms who are considering abortion respond, "Oh, I could never do that to my child" when adoption is suggested. Nevertheless, in turn they hand their children over to day care when they are little, and state day care once they've reached schooling age.

Please don't misunderstand how we do school in the context of life. It starts with life, rather than school. When I call out to my children, "Daddy's got to run something off to the printer. Who wants to come with me?" I'm not thinking, "I didn't get math drills done today. I'll be extra efficient and do it while driving." No, instead I want to enjoy conversation with my children. (By the way, I use my car stereo only when I'm driving alone.) Our reward? A joyful conversation, a delight.

It's not unusual when driving with my children for me to remind them, given the beauty of our little corner of the planet, "Hasn't God blessed us in allowing us to live in such a beautiful place?" Or I will tell the smaller children, "Look at the beautiful mountains God made." This is not Sunday school, and neither is it aesthetics class. It's simple conversation. What do my children learn? They learn to look at their world in light of God's sovereignty, in light of his beauty. Is that enough? Is that an education? Of course it is.

Once more the devil and the angel are dancing on my shoulders. I'm not suggesting that you may never sit your child down at a desk. My own children do indeed enjoy more formal times of learning, especially considering their youth. Instead I'm hoping we'll come to understand that there is no line that separates life from school.

I have to wonder again, how different the world might be if we acted on our conviction that the Bible is the Word of God, if God's people were in the habit of interpreting everything in light of that Word. How might we teach our children if we loved and delighted in God's Word and in his world? We talk to our children when they lie down and when they rise up, we speak to them of who God is and how he relates to his world—that is how we develop a Christian worldview. It doesn't come from reading worldview books, going to worldview camps, or taking worldview classes. Our children will adopt a Christian worldview as we talk to them about God and how he relates to everything. That's how we raise up godly seed.

THE THREE Gs

4

We began our journey in understanding the proper education of our covenant children by looking at the goal of education. We affirmed that no matter how clever or hardworking
we might be, if our goal is not the Bible's goal, then we cannot do well. Then we talked about the who of education, how
God calls parents to be about the business of training up children in the nurture and admonition of the Lord. We suggested
that it is parents alone who will answer before God for the education they provide for their children. In the previous chapter we talked about how our lack of faith causes us to construct
elaborate schemes for the how of education. We just can't believe it could be as simple as God lays out in Deuteronomy 6.
Conversation can't be the answer, we think, because that doesn't
involve an expensive and elaborate infrastructure or curricula designed by experts.

Of all the ways that we fail to believe God on the theme of education, we believe him least about this chapter's subject: the proper content of education. The world has so shaped our thinking on education that the content of our children's education needs a thorough reformation. Why are we so out of line? Simply, we are as far off as we are because the state schools are as far off as they are. Many homeschoolers, rightly appalled at the sewage being taught at the local state school, take their children out of that environment but end up too easily pleased because they've removed some sewage. However, making homeschools better than state schools isn't a particularly grand accomplishment.

I have a dear friend who was educated at Christian schools all her life, save for one year. (Christian schools, by the way, suffer from the same problem of inadequately reforming the state's curriculum.) That one year she attended the local state school. Before long, she was significantly affected by being in that state school. I remember how my friend became a committed environmentalist, just as her school's teachers planned. Her parents are Christians, committed conservatives. But she came home affirming that it was a good thing for the state to force people to do this and that for the environment. She was just one short step from asserting, as some radical environmentalists do, "Meat is murder." Her parents were appalled, and the next year my friend was back in the Christian school.

There she was not taught that man is a cancer on the planet. She was not taught that man had emerged from the primordial ooze, the product of an accidental collision of time, energy, and chance. She did not read the paradigmatic state-school reader, *Heather Has Two Mommies*, a sweet peek into fictional Heather's lesbian household. (There is a male version as well, *Daddy's New Roommate*.) She didn't have her values "clarified." (She did, however, come close. A junior-high English text at this conservative Christian school explained one way you can tell the difference between a fact and an opinion: opinions often contain words like *should* and *ought*. So "You should obey your parents" is no longer a fact but a mere opinion.) She wasn't taught radical feminism either.

The trouble is, even when we succeed in getting rid of all that worldly stuff that offends our sensibilities, even when we get rid of what assaults our worldview, we still haven't answered the question, "What then should we teach?" You can't determine what should be taught to your children simply by taking away what should not be taught to your children. Nor is it sufficient to simply be reactionary. If they have classes on evolution, we'll have classes on creation. If they have classes on feminism, we will have classes on femininity. If they have classes on environmentalism, we'll have classes on dominion. That approach still has the state determining what we will teach our children.

In short, it's not enough to beat the other guy. In my book *Tearing Down Strongholds*, I make arguments against a series of unbelieving epistemologies (or systems for how we determine what is true). Making unbelievers look foolish isn't such a difficult thing to do, since the Bible tells us, "The fool has said in his heart, 'There is no God'" (Ps. 14:1). The logical positivist argues that only those statements that can be empirically verified (that is, demonstrated through our senses) have any meaning. But the statement, "Only those statements that can be empirically verified have any meaning" cannot be verified empirically and so is by its own standard nonsense. When the relativist argues, "There is no such thing as objective truth," we hoist him on his own petard by asking, "Is it objectively true that there is no such thing as objective truth?" It can be great fun to expose folly. But it does nothing toward establishing truth. That's another game altogether. Tossing stuff out does nothing to put anything in.

Certainly what is left isn't as morally repugnant as what was tossed. But our goal isn't simply to have a curriculum that isn't morally repugnant. Too often what is left, while being "clean," is beside the point. All of this goes back to chapter 1. We teach the wrong content because we have the wrong goals. The state is intent on making our children into faithful servants of the state. It wants to turn our children into one-world socialist liberals. Homeschoolers, too often I'm afraid, rightly have a different goal, but their goal is still wrong. They homeschool because they want their children to grow up to be conservative Republicans. When you toss Heather's two mommies overboard, when you ditch the feminism and the environmentalism, what you have left is Republicanism. To be sure, you'll probably make a Republican who is better than most Republicans. But this ought not to be our goal.

When we ask what our goal ought to be, we need to carefully see what we have borrowed from the world. Our tendency, since the time of the Enlightenment, is to look at ethical questions like, "What ought I to be teaching my children?" in a sort of scientific way. We reduce the issues down to abstractions, put them in some computer, and out comes the answer. When you study ethics in college or in graduate school, you are presented with a list of varying theories. You learn about utilitarianism and its various versions. You learn about deontological ethics. You learn about Joseph Fletcher's understanding of situation ethics. Then these theories fight it out, or worse, everyone agrees that there is no right answer and embraces ethical relativism. What you don't often get is what I like to call an agrarian approach to ethics, an approach that is earthier, more natural. It is an approach that dismisses the abstract out of hand, because ethics is all about how we are to live. The real question we need to ask is not which theory has the most going for it, but this simple question—what is the good life?

My guess is that if you are reading this book and God has blessed you with children, you love those children. But what does it mean to love your children? What does it mean in terms of your hopes for them? I would suggest that, given the common grace of God (the remnants of the image of God left in all mankind), virtually all parents, whether committed Christians, atheists, Muslims, or Mormons, want their children to live the good life. What separates these parents of different faiths is not whether they want their children to live the good life, but what their conception of the good life is. Our problem as Christians is we don't ask this fundamental question, "What is the good life?" We simply absorb the world's vision of the good life. We live in the pursuit of personal peace and affluence, and we train and equip our children to do the same. Our decisions on the content of our children's education are based on this pursuit. We want to make sure that our children are given what is necessary to succeed in their pursuit of personal peace and affluence. What separates us from unbelievers on this count is simply that we add to our goal the hope that our children make a profession of faith, not falling into any gross or heinous sin along the way.

It's not unusual for me to engage in debates. What is interesting about so many of them is the depth to which the disagreement goes. We can't agree on x because we don't agree about the good life. For example, my friends recently had a baby. Elizabeth was born in the hospital, a healthy little girl. When it was time for baby and mommy to leave the hospital, their doctor (another friend) signed all the release papers, and told them they could go. After the doctor left, however, the nurses descended upon the family, insisting that the baby first needed this test and that, and couldn't be released yet. My friend reminded the nurses that the doctor had approved their departure. He suggested that whatever misunderstanding there was, perhaps it should be worked out between them and the doctor. They spoke to the doctor and came up with a compromise. The family and the baby could go, but only after signing assorted papers declaring they were leaving "against medical advice." My friend rightly complained, "My doctor said we could go. Whose advice are we not listening to?"

Finally they were released, the nurse wheeling mom and baby to their car. The nurse, however, didn't warmly send them on their way, encouraging them to love that baby. Instead she watched officiously as my friends put Elizabeth into the baby car seat. The father postulated that the reason a nurse comes to the car with families is precisely to make sure they put their babies in proper car seats. (Some hospitals even offer new parents an approved child-safety seat with each child they have— a rather nicer way of ensuring the baby gets home safely.)

Out of this story came a three-way argument. My friend had a friend who could not understand why he was put out by the intrusiveness of the state on this matter. From there the conversation went on to relative merits of relative amounts of intrusiveness. What surprised me was the argument my friend's friend made against my view. He argued, "If the state were as unobtrusive as you seem to want, why, we wouldn't even have driver's licenses or building permits." This was presented in a tone of unmitigated horror. I could only horrify my opponent further by explaining, "Such a world doesn't scare me; it excites me. My idea of a happy place and an appropriately limited government would be one without building permits and without driver's licenses." We had two different visions of what the good life is. But we have an impeccable source for telling us what the good life is. We will find it in our Bibles, once more back in Deuteronomy:

Now this is the commandment, and these are the statutes and judgments which the LORD your God has commanded to teach you, that you may observe them in the land which you are crossing over to possess, that you may fear the LORD your God, to keep all His statutes and His commandments which I command you, you and your son and your grandson, all the days of your life, and that your days may be prolonged. Therefore hear, O Israel, and be careful to observe it, that it may be well with you, and that you may multiply greatly as the LORD God of your fathers has promised you—"a land flowing with milk and honey." Hear, O Israel: The LORD our God, the LORD is one! You shall love the LORD your God with all your heart, with all your soul, and with all your strength. And these words which I command you today shall be in your heart. You shall teach them diligently to your children, and shall talk of them when you sit in your house, when you walk by the way, when you lie down, and when you rise up. You shall bind them as a sign on your hand, and they shall be as frontlets between your eyes. You shall write them on the doorposts of your house and on your gates. (Deut. 6:1–9)

When I was still in seminary, we had a rather peculiar way of studying books of the Bible. Too often, the professor would spend an hour or so talking about what liberal theologians had to say about the book at hand, when it was written, and by whom. The professor would talk about the best commentaries on the book and the commentaries best

84

avoided. We would cover who the book was written to and in what context it was written. It used to drive me crazy. I stifled the urge to shout, "But what does the book say? Can we talk about the actual message here? I'm far more concerned about what God wanted to communicate than I am about what some unbeliever thinks of this book."

The truth is that while some of those concerns don't help in understanding the text, some are rather important. Context is critical to understanding any text, inerrant or not. And context includes issues of audience, author, and occasion. Here in Deuteronomy we know, contra the liberals, that our earthly author is Moses. What we may forget is more of the context. This book is essentially Moses' farewell sermon. He is not simply leaving one pastorate to go take a bigger congregation in a bigger city. Rather, he is saying goodbye to a people whom he has loved and served for decades. The Book of Deuteronomy is Moses' last word to the nation of Israel before he dies, and before they go into the Promised Land. That is the context. But stop and think for a moment about Moses' life. Imagine being the political, the military, the administrative, the theological, and the pastoral leader of God's people. That is a heavy burden, a great weight. So heavy, in fact, that at one point Moses pleads with God to kill him, so that he might escape the burden. As a pastor I can understand Moses' frustration, which is grounded in something that may surprise you. The problem wasn't that every time Moses sat down for supper the phone rang with some petty pastoral issue. The problem wasn't his low salary. The problem wasn't administrative chores that were not a part of his biblical calling (but were a part of the congregation's vision of how things have always been done). Moses' complaint was that he couldn't manage such a stiff-necked and rebellious people. He cared too much for these people, and it hurt him to his core when they acted in such foolish and self-destructive ways.

Moses isn't trying to even the score. He isn't saying, "Now that my death is just around the corner, and now that you won't have me to kick around anymore, let me tell you what I really think of you." Instead the picture here is of a father saying farewell to two million of his beloved children. He is instructing them one last time, expressing his desire that it will go well for them in the land God gives them, in a land flowing with milk and honey.

This ought to shape how we understand this passage. Moses is not simply being a stern father, warning his children to do this or expect the wrath of God. Nor is he simply giving side instructions, telling the folks, "When you, in your own wisdom and power, are about the business of pursuing the good life, don't forget about these things." Nor is he saying, "These things will serve as a broad hedge to pen you in while you, in your own strength and wisdom, pursue the good life." No, this command is the good life. Moses is telling the children of Israel (and, through them, us) that the good life is knowing, believing, and acting upon what I call the Three Gs. The Three Gs are the very content of a biblical homeschool.

The first G should be rather obvious. The first thing we need to be teaching our children, that they may have a good life, is "Who is God?" Jesus himself, in his high priestly prayer, made much the same point: "And this is eternal life, that they may know You, the only true God, and Jesus Christ whom You have sent" (John 17:3). Our problem is that when we come to passages like this we think, "If I didn't have God, all this personal peace and affluence I've won wouldn't be nearly as good." Indeed, we think knowing God is a means to attaining greater peace and affluence, turning God into a means and showing that we don't know him. God's message isn't that he's a help to the good life, but that knowing him is the very being of life. Knowing him isn't what makes life better, nor what protects life—knowing him is life.

When we forget this, when knowing God is just something we do on Sunday, something secondary, we prove ourselves to be (and, worse, train our children to be) idolaters. Seeking anything outside knowing who God is means it won't go well with them in the land. But the point, remember, isn't that if you worship God and you know who he is, he will in turn be nice to you so that you can live the good life. Living the good life *is* knowing God. David writes, "The LORD is my shepherd; I shall not want" (Ps. 23:1). No mention of green grass or still waters yet. David is satisfied simply to have God as his shepherd. The good life is knowing God.

Not too long ago I participated in a recorded discussion of worship titled, "The Queen of Days." We chose that title precisely because we want to see how set apart the Lord's Day is. The Lord's Day is the Queen of Days. Why? We know God is always with us. We know that we are to rejoice and be glad in each day the Lord has made. Every day is a holy day. But on every Lord's Day God renews covenant with us, he meets with us, and we see him more clearly. We get to be closer to him because his Spirit lifts us up to the heavenly Mount Zion (see Heb. 12). That's the climax of our week. If that's not it, if that's not the queen, the climax, the summation of the good life, then God is just a prop or a hedge or a buttress.

What has this to do with homeschooling? Everything. Because when we homeschool we must teach our children who God is, and in so doing we teach them the good life. That in turn is our satisfaction, our fulfillment, our joy. We want our children to know God because we love them.

My son Campbell and I met recently for our Bible study. We meet once or twice a week. Our focus of late has been the Book of Proverbs. My heart's desire for him is that he would be a boy, and one day a man, equipped with wisdom. So I explained to him, "Wisdom, Son, is knowing how much to value things." Our family plays a simple game called the punch-buggy game when we drive somewhere. The goal is to be the first to spot a Volkswagen Beetle. If you see one, you name the color and cry out "White punch buggy" or "Green punch buggy." Now, in many families' practice, punches are involved. Some games, I'm sure, involve ungracious punches. Other games, I'm sure, involve gentle punches given by children with a high degree of self-control. We have opted to remove the whole punching part of the game because our children had trouble being sufficiently gentle. All we do is keep track of who spotted how many, and the one with the most at the end of a trip wins.

My son is gifted in this game. He knows where the parked punch buggies are, and always gets them first. He also keeps his eyes peeled in every direction. We had gone to get haircuts one day, and he dominated me. He beat me three to nothing on the way to the haircut, and five to nothing on the way home. But there are times when his sisters get the punch buggies before he does. Sometimes my son can be a bit on the competitive side. I don't know where he gets it. But he's been known to get upset when his sisters beat him in this game. During our Bible study I explained to him about wisdom. "Son," I said, "I don't mind you enjoying this game. It's fun and is a gift from God. But it should not mean so much to you. That's not wise. That's elevating it to a place where it doesn't belong. Knowing God is the thing we want. If you want to be upset about something, be upset that you don't yet know God better, not that your little sister saw the blue punch buggy before you did."

The same is true for all of us. I'm ashamed of the petty things that concern me. When the Pittsburgh Steelers lose a football game, it bothers me. Isn't that the silliest thing? I'm not nearly concerned enough with my own knowledge of God, with my own sanctification. I worry about what other people think of me, rather than about my thoughts about God. We all have folly to lose.

Our calling is to tell our children who God is. This doesn't stop, of course, once they have made a decision for Christ. This is our eternity, that we will know him better and better on into eternity. When we wake up each morning, we ought not ask ourselves, "How can I prepare my child to enter into the nice middle-class world of grown-ups?" Rather, we should be asking, "How do I tell my children who God is?"

How do you teach your children who God is? One important and biblical way is through the second G. We tell our children, "What has God done?" Our tendency is to look at the character of God and see it in abstract terms. We think we're seeking clarity, but too often we lose it. I remember being asked by one of my professors in seminary, "Does God have a strong right arm?" I was puzzled by the question, assuming that the professor and I would certainly be on the same page here. Finally, I had to speak the obvious: "No, God doesn't have a strong right arm. The Bible says God is spirit." My professor, no doubt pleased that I had stepped into his trap, replied, "The Bible also says that God has a strong right arm." "Well," I explained, "that's anthropomorphic language. What it means is that God is omnipotent." "But the Bible says," the professor concluded enigmatically, "that God has a strong right arm." The bell rang, ending our little tussle, and it wasn't until years later that I began to see something of my professor's point. There is content in "strong right arm" that is missing from the theologically correct "omnipotent." Both speak of strength, but the former maintains a personal angle. The former implies that this strength is used for the protection and well-being of the people of God. The latter sounds more like a wattage listing for a microwave oven.

God is not merely like a string of pearls, each attribute set apart on its own. He is the God who acts, the God who is there and is not silent. We teach our children who God is as we teach them what he has done for his people. Here we need to be careful. I'm afraid in our attempt to make the Bible more accessible to little children that we may have given the devil a foothold. When our children's Bible storybooks come equipped with cartoon pictures of David, Abraham, and Noah, it is very easy for the children to think of these heroes of the faith as cartoon characters. Instead they need to understand that because we are now the children of Abraham, that this is our family story.

Once again the devil and the angel are dancing on my shoulders. Am I saying you can never teach your children phonics? Before I answer, let me give a little diagnostic test. We may come to understand our own overall motives better if we ask ourselves, "Why do we teach our children to read?" It's a question too few of us think about. Keep in mind that for millennia God raised up godly men and women who could neither read nor write. I'm afraid most people, if they are honest, would explain that their children need to learn how to read so they can get a good job. That is, it's a tool for personal peace and affluence. Some others might suggest that they want their children to be able to read so they can participate in the "great conversation." If they can read, then they can interact with Pliny and Boethius, with Kant and Hume. Still others might say, "Just for the joy of it." I like to read, and I want my children to enjoy the same pleasure. In fact, my two oldest are reading right now, and I wish I could be reading with them.

Then there are those Presbyterian parents, people in my

own tradition, who want their children to learn to read so they can read all of Paul's epistles and really get their theology down. On its face this is a good thing, but only because it is part of how we learn the greater thing, who God is, and what he has done. The good life is knowing God's story, which certainly includes Paul's epistles, but likewise includes a great deal more. There is more to the story than justification and predestination. Not less, but more. We ought to teach our children to read so that they can know God better.

The first G is "Who is God?" The second G is much like the first, "What has God done?" The third and final G is "What does God require?" Moses said to his people, "These words which I command you today shall be on your heart and you shall teach them diligently to your children. . . ." What words? What is the antecedent to "these words" in the context here? What is it that Moses wants them not to forget?

I would suggest that he is telling them they must not lose sight of what I call the Quadrateuch, the first four books of the Bible, which will become the Pentateuch once he has finished this last sermon. Moses is warning them not to forget all that he has already told them in the books he has written and is writing. His teachings go back to the beginning of time. You teach your children history, all the way back to the beginning that Moses wrote about. You teach your children the dreadful glory of the creation, God speaking all things into being. You tell them the story from Adam to Moses, all of which tells us who God is. But then, in the books of Leviticus and Deuteronomy, Moses gives us the very law of God. We are told what God requires of us. In these first five books we are told who God is, what God has done, and what God requires. We learn, in short, God's covenant with his people.

Even here, however, even when addressing what God requires of us, we find a way to separate his wisdom from the good life. We are syncretists, blending together the worship of the true and living God with the worship of personal peace and affluence. And this is how we divvy up the worship pie. We cut God this deal: "Lord, we know you are the master of all things. We know that you are the lawgiver. So what we are going to do, while we worship personal peace and affluence, we're going to serve that god in accordance with your law. You will give us ethics, but the other god will give us purpose. We will pursue the world's vision of the good life, but we'll pursue it without stealing or committing adultery. We'll pursue it, but we'll be sure to pay our tithes along the way."

But you cannot separate the law of God from the true good life. Think of it in terms of your marriage. We know that God commands husbands to love their wives. And lest we become all sentimental, we rush in to emphasize that love isn't a warm, gooshy feeling. Nope, we remind ourselves, it's service. That's an important point. Love is active, a decision, more a behavior than a feeling. But let's not fall off the other side of the horse. Loving one's wife isn't an unpleasant thing. It is the good life to look at one's spouse and think, "Oh my stars, but the grace of God is overwhelming." When we have a child, we cry precisely because we are overcome with the joy of the good life, the real deal. You don't have six children so that you can pursue personal peace and affluence—trust me. But what you find out is that this is the richest thing you can have. The law is the good life. When we are teaching it to our children, we are directing them in the paths they should go.

God promises that he will reward obedience. And he certainly will. But there is another sense in which obedience is its own reward. Here we get confused as well. We think "Obedience is its own reward" means that when we do the right thing, we feel so warm inside that it was all worth it. It is deeper than that. Obedience is the good life. The law of God is designed to match us as we are. As we obey, we are right with the world. That is one more glory of the law of God. It is not a set of rules designed to frustrate us, but a series of directions designed to liberate us. And it can all be summarized with the mandate to exercise dominion.

What are you supposed to teach your children? To exercise dominion for God's glory. Now we are back to our methodology. That is, if all our days are about the exercise of dominion, then we are always in school. Let's try a little quiz. When my daughter Darby is giving table scraps to our chickens, is she (a) learning obedience and hard work, (b) doing school, (c) living the good life, (d) exercising dominion, (e) humoring her daddy's silly dream of succeeding with the chickens, or (f) all of the above? I trust the answer is obvious.

God calls us in Deuteronomy 6, through the prophet Moses, to teach our children who he is, what he has done, and what he requires. But remember that he didn't stop revealing himself at the close of Deuteronomy. Neither did he stop acting then, nor did he stop speaking law. That is, Moses' command applies first to the entire Bible. The whole Bible is our family story, showing us our heavenly Father and telling us what he would have us do.

There is still more. For God did not cease to act with the closing of the canon. No battle rages between the angel and the devil on my shoulders here. One might argue that the Book of Acts doesn't ultimately describe the acts of the apostles, but rather describes the acts of Christ through the apostles. But he didn't stop at the end of Acts. Jesus is even now about the business of making all his enemies his footstool. He is not only active in human history, but also Lord over that history, since he is the one who wields all authority in heaven and on earth. History, rightly understood, is his story. His story covers everything from Genesis to today's paper, to the really important information, like the notice in the church bulletin about somebody's baptism. It's all his, and therefore is precisely what we should be teaching our children.

If you teach the Three Gs, you will likewise be teaching what you have been learning. That is, what God requires is that we teach our children to teach their children what God requires. If we want to see homeschooling thrive and grow, not just in numbers but also in obedience, if we want to pass the first great test, it will be when the first generation of homeschooled children have their own children. We are doomed to fail if we do not teach our children why we teach our children, so that they in turn will teach our grandchildren. Teaching the children who God is, what God has done, and what God requires is the center of covenantal succession, and the center of homeschooling.

If you are like me, you long to see your children exceed you in holiness. You want your grandchildren to do still better. If you're like me, you look for progressive familial sanctification, one generation standing on the shoulders of the previous generation and seeing further into the consummation of the kingdom. For this to happen takes one thing: homeschooling biblically, which includes teaching our children to homeschool biblically. We don't start with the state's curriculum, and then attempt to find a Bible passage to justify each part. Rather, we start with the Bible and go from there, learning evermore of who God is, of what he has done, and of what he requires of us.

BOYS AND GIRLS

5

In our previous chapter we considered together what we call, in professional, inorganic, industrial terms, "curricula." That is, we talked about what we are called to teach our children. We had, as with the chapters before that, some hard things to say. We found that there was still folly left from the world in our thinking about education. This chapter will be little different. We will have some hard things to say.

There is, understandably, a great deal of overlap between what we're supposed to be teaching our boys and what we're supposed to be teaching our girls. Both of them will serve the same God, know the same history. Both of them bear the same image of God. They are equal in dignity and value. But they will be called to different roles, and so once more, _contra mundum,_ we affirm that there is a difference in what they should be taught. There ought not to be a one-size-fits-all approach that denies the differences in boys and girls.

The Three Gs, which all—boys and girls, men and women—need to know and study for all our lives, must be understood in their biblical context. They need to be learned in the context of the antithesis. What is antithesis? Such a fancy term has a pretty basic meaning. It's us versus the world. We remember that after Adam and Eve ate of the forbidden fruit, God pronounced a curse on each. But he also cursed the serpent, saying, "Because you have done this, you are cursed more than all cattle, and more than every beast of the field; on your belly you shall go, and you shall eat dust all the days of your life. I will put enmity between you and the woman, and between your seed and her Seed; He shall bruise your head, and you shall bruise His heel" (Gen. 3:14–15). Here God declares solemn war against the serpent, and not only promises to destroy the serpent through one born of a woman, but also promises to change the hearts of his elect, such that they would hate the serpent. This great battle is the setting of history, and therefore the setting of our lives. If we are his, we are at war, and that affects everything.

One of the serpent's most potent weapons in this great war is to entice us to forget the war. He has even had a measure of success in the homeschool movement. Once, not too long ago, homeschooling was so unusual, so countercultural, that one had to be self-consciously fighting the folly of this world to adopt it. Not so anymore. Now homeschooling has become safe, mainstream, comfortable, and thus we have lost much of the antithesis. Consider what happened in Alaska just a few short years ago. The state legislature there passed a charter-school law that was rather appealing to homeschoolers. The concept of charter schools is pretty simple. The state, hoping to foster competition and innovation, offers to finance a school with public funds, without exercising the kind of overbearing oversight it would exercise over a regular state school. The state pays (with taxes) while private companies run the charter schools.

Alaska determined that homeschools could be considered charter schools. Thus the state would pay the expenses of the homeschool, for textbooks and equipment, if the homeschooling family would do two things. First, they had to register their homeschool as a charter school. And second, they had to use approved texts in the school, texts that were religiously "neutral." It seems the state of Alaska, in trying to slow down homeschooling, decided to try the carrot rather than the stick. And they succeeded, as three-fourths of homeschoolers opted for this choice. These folks aren't thinking in antithetical terms. Instead they are thinking in Judas terms. They decided to toss Jesus out of the texts, get a check, and make Caesar happy all in one fell swoop. These parents, sadly, don't see education in light of the battle between the seed of the woman and the seed of the serpent.

Too often the children are the same. Too many homeschooled children lack a zeal for antithesis, for thinking in these biblical categories. I'm not saying homeschoolers as a rule are worldly. I haven't experienced that as yet. Homeschooled children tend to be more modest. They tend to have more gentle and quiet spirits. They tend to be more articulate, all of which is good. You don't see many with baggy pants drooping around their knees, or sporting bare midriffs like the pop stars of our age. That's all good, but it's not enough, it's not success if our children merely succeed in being clean-cut. It's not even enough for them to profess faith in Christ. What we want from these children, male and female, is a commitment to being Christian soldiers, who are always thinking in terms of the antithesis. We want warriors who understand that Satan wants them to think as he does, who know what's going on in the world, and who care with a passion, with zeal. That's what I mean by a zeal for antithesis. Instead I find too often a propensity among homeschoolers to be somewhat blasé about what's wrong with the world. They seem to think, "Yeah, well, that's what the world's like."

This pattern is consistent with the cocoon accusation that is often leveled against those who homeschool. One reason it is so important to remember that our lives are lived in the context of the war being waged by Christ against the serpent is that it reminds us that the serpent is waging war with us. And, by and large, the weapons of his warfare are not carnal either. His goal is to get us to see the world as he sees it, to think his thoughts after him. To the degree that homeschooled children are unaware that such is the devil's game, he wins at his game. Homeschoolers lack a fitting dread that they might be conformed to this world.

Too often we are guilty of an unhealthy sheltering.

(Clearly, there is an appropriate kind of sheltering. When those who are opposed to homeschooling accuse me of sheltering my children, my reply is always, "What are you going to accuse me of next, feeding and clothing them?") We sometimes keep our children from what is going on in the world, and we even keep them from what is going on in the Bible (which, truth be told, would certainly garner an R rating). They need to know these things, without making them live in the gutter. They need to be aware of the worldviews around them.

Not long ago my oldest daughter described someone to me, saying, "So-and-so sounds like a feminist." Now, my daughter doesn't hang around with Erica Jong and Gloria Steinem. The women she knows best are homeschooling moms from her church community. She certainly has never suffered the slings and arrows of an angry feminist telling her to get down in the sludge and start acting like a boy. But she knows what and how feminists think.

Darby watches me as I instill a sound worldview in her younger siblings. One evening I was reading a book to Erin Claire. It was a fairly typical children's book, in that it invited children to imagine themselves in a host of different jobs, and explained what each job might be like. A page or two featured astronauts and firemen. One part really stood out: "Imagine if you were a millionaire . . ." as if being a millionaire were some sort of job one could get. Then it went on to say, "You would be lucky that you have more than you need." However, Erin Claire heard me translate on the fly, "You would have been very blessed by God. Isn't that wonderful?" Darby knew that I had changed the words, so I asked her, "Do you get to be a millionaire by being lucky?" "No, Daddy," she replied, "but that's what the silly people who made that book think." The point is not this particular lesson, but that we need not be afraid to teach our children these things.

Just about every night during family worship, and probably every night in her own prayers, Darby asks for us to pray that the president would be a godly president. She prayed this as well in the previous administration. There are, of course, a number of things that would be different if the president were a more godly man. But Darby knows the most important one would be for the president to fight to outlaw abortion. There may be no sin more ugly than abortion. And my children have never seen *The Silent Scream*, a video of a live abortion, or a diagram of a partial-birth abortion. They don't know how these things are done. But they do know that we live in a country where over a million women every year hire doctors to murder their babies before they are born.

The children know what it looks like when a country turns its back on God, for they've read it in their Bibles. They know what happened in John's gospel, when the Jewish leaders rejected their king and chose Rome instead. They weren't faithful, and God judged them in their infidelity. That happens, and it can happen to us. That's why we teach them the lesson. In fact, because my children learn from the Bible, and from history, they are often told, "You know, many times the state becomes terribly wicked. And when that happens, sometimes they come after people like you and me."

Why are our children protected from these hard truths? Why don't they have such a profound sense of the antithesis? My guess is that it's because their teachers don't have a deep and profound sense of the antithesis. Our children do not look at the lost as the enemy (whom, by the way, we are called to love in the midst of battle) because we don't look at the lost as the enemy. We think they're just "lost," people just like us who are missing some directions. We confuse innocence with ignorance, and then we confuse knowledge with sin. We say we want our children to be innocent, but what we mean is we don't want them on guard against the attacks of the enemy, just like Eve. And when they fall into the attacks of sin, we reason, "The problem is they know stuff." We forget that the problem isn't knowing stuff; the problem is loving sin. By not wanting our children to lose their "innocence," we treat the hard truths about sin in the world the way we treat the hard truth that there is no Santa Claus. It's nice to live in a world where a jolly man in a red suit comes down your chimney. And it's nice to live in a world where everybody gets along and nobody has any different views.

   •   But there's another reason, another slight error we make. It is good and right that we don't want our children to be scared. When we were working our way through the Book of Acts during family worship, almost every night the application of whatever text we covered was some version of, "They might come one day; you better be faithful. Don't you betray Jesus, even if it means torture and death." And my saintly wife, understandably, was a little concerned. "Do you think it's wise?" she asked. "These poor children aren't going to be able to sleep at night." How should I answer that? Should I tell the children, the next time we read about a martyr, "It's not really that bad. This could never happen to you or to your children"?

No, instead I teach them to find comfort in the same place the people in Acts found comfort, in the sovereignty of God, or in his strong right arm. The counterbalance is in the power of God and his promises. If enemies come and take us away, that's okay. What's the worst they can do? To live is Christ, and to die is gain. They can't take anything from us, for our treasure is in heaven. If they do come, let us rejoice to be counted among his martyrs. Our children need to know the glory and the beauty of heaven, to long for a better country, to know that their citizenship is in heaven alone. They need to understand that the war they are in is all too real, but at the same time, that they are safe. Yea, though they walk through the valley of the shadow of death, they ought to fear no evil, for God is with them. They need to know that the Jesus they serve is already sovereign, so that if bad guys come, it is only because the one Good Guy ordained it for our good and for his glory.

It didn't take Moses' explaining Genesis 3 to the children of Israel for them to understand the antithesis. They lived the antithesis. God had rescued them from the Egyptians, a group of people that were more than merely lost. When God called his people out of Egypt, the Egyptians didn't quietly acquiesce. But there was more history the children of Israel needed to learn. They lived through the failure of their fathers at the golden calf. The lesson? <u>Death comes to those who seek to join together that which is of God and that which is of the devil</u>. Every Hebrew child had to learn: were they going to be like the faithful Levites that put to death the idolaters, or would they be like the idolaters that were put to death?

Even after the life of Moses, we see much the same thing. After God has given the people the land of promise, Joshua gathers them together at Shechem. They are gathered there to renew covenant, to remember that they must keep covenant, and that they must teach their children the covenant. The children of Israel are to remember what God did to Achan and his family for taking the accursed thing. They are to remember how God delivered them at Jericho, and brought into his fold the family of Rahab.

None of these hard truths, however, are presented in lurid detail. We don't need to turn the stomachs of our children by describing in great detail what the water pressure would have done to the Egyptian soldiers when the Red Sea came back together. We don't have to describe for them the details of the process of stoning that Achan went through. <u>But we do need to let our children know they live in the context of this war, and real things happen in it to real people.</u> Our children need to understand both the <u>identity</u> of <u>their enemies</u> (again whom they are called to love) <u>and their own identity.</u> They are a part of the kingdom of God, brought in by the grace of God.

Both boys and girls need to know these things, since both are warriors in this great battle. They need to know of the strong right arm of their great commander. They also need to learn the lesson of the three brave youths in the account of Daniel. Shadrach, Meshach, and Abednego, having refused to bow down before the golden image of the king, are brought to the fiery furnace. Nebuchadnezzar said, "If you do not worship, you shall be cast immediately into the midst of a burning fiery furnace. And who is the god who will deliver you from my hands?" (Dan. 3:15). The young men didn't exhibit false bravado. They didn't try to bind God's hands. Their answer is one of both humility and trust. "Shadrach, Meshach, and Abed-Nego answered and said to the king, 'O Nebuchadnezzar, we have no need to answer you in this matter. If that is the case, our God whom we serve is able to deliver us from the burning fiery furnace, and He will deliver us from your hand, O king. But if not, let it be known to you, O king, that we do not serve your gods, nor will we worship the gold image which you have set up" (Dan. 3:16–18). Confidence in his sovereignty doesn't mean assurance that we will not die at the hands of God's enemies.

The same has happened since the completion of the Bible. Just as we have argued that God continues to act in history, so has he been pleased with the death of his saints through martyrdom. Our children, boys and girls, need to know of their forbears in Scotland, the Covenanters who were put to death for their faith. They need to know of the massacre of the Huguenots in France on Saint Bartholomew's Day. Whenever parents teach history, they are giving sermons. We must apply the lessons learned from these stories. That's how we teach history, how we speak of these things when our children rise up and when they lie down.

Because homeschooling is done in the context of life, it changes as life changes. Recently my dear wife was giving me a report on how my eldest was doing with her math. (See, we do do math.) My wife was shocked that Darby read the lesson, and then did the work. She taught Darby to read, and now Darby is learning her math. But that's not how she started learning her math. When she was very little we would drill math while running errands together. I'd strap her in her car seat, and as we drove to town ask her, "What is one plus one?" I have continued to teach the children math through this process. When our children are sent to bed, they are given time with lights on to read or look at books. When I would come to turn out their lights, I sometimes would drill the children on their math. I would lie down with Campbell and go through his addition. I would do the same with Delaney. Darby went through her multiplication tables with me in this way. They have learned their math rather literally, "when they lie down."

But as they've gotten older, as they have progressed somewhat closer to what the classical model calls the logic stage, it becomes more and more worldview time. (Of course, it is always worldview time. The grammar of worldview is simply telling the children who are the good guys and who the bad. We establish their loyalties while they are yet young. This is part of what it means to raise our children in the nurture and admonition of the Lord.) When we teach worldview, we again

WHEN YOU RISE UP

do it in the context of real life. We don't have a "worldview" book, unless you count the Bible. We don't have a "worldview" curriculum, unless you count the conversations we have. Sometimes lessons come about through the day's news. I will tell the children about something I heard on the radio. One day I heard a story about a high school student in Florida whose family was in the process of moving from one home to another. The girl was the valedictorian of her class. During the move, she stuck a box or two of things in her car. A kitchen knife fell out of one of the boxes and got stuck in the carpet underneath the back seat of the car. Someone spotted the offending "weapon." The girl was suspended from school, and lost her valedictorian status. I encouraged my children to consider how this story illustrates the biblical principle, "The wicked flee though no one pursues." It's always lesson time, for both boys and girls.

Having established that not only all of education, but all of life is lived in the context of antithesis, having affirmed that there are no noncombatants in this war, that everyone—boys and girls, mothers and fathers—fights, we do have to concede that different people have different roles to play in this great battle. Both sexes fight, but they fight in different ways. Both sexes do not have carnal weapons, but both sexes fight. It's especially important for men to get that. In some sense, the war is out there. We want our homes to be havens of peace. We want our wives to be a part of that peaceful haven. All of that is well and good. But it doesn't mean our wives are not at war.

We raise our daughters to be warriors for the kingdom

by raising them to be keepers at home. Remember that back in the garden there is, in a sense, a twofold element to the dominion mandate. Adam and Eve (who, you will remember, was made to be a help to Adam in his charge to exercise dominion) are supposed not only to exercise dominion, but dress and keep the garden. God had given them a model of the end product in the Garden of Eden. They were both to protect that model, and to reshape the outlying jungle to reflect the glory of the garden. Adam, being the head of the household, was responsible for the whole enterprise. (Some say, in fact, that he sinned in not guarding Eve in the garden.) But, being masculine, his focus would tend to be more outward. He would go into the jungle and gardenize it. Eve, being feminine, called to be a keeper at home, would focus on keeping the garden. He is outward-looking, while she is inward-looking. He is aggressive; she is protective.

But remember that this is warfare. Consider what Paul says in Titus 2: "Older women likewise are to be reverent in behavior, not slanderers or slaves to much wine. They are to teach what is good, and so train the young women to love their husbands and children, to be self-controlled, pure, working at home, kind, and submissive to their own husbands..." (Titus 2:3-5a). Though much of the church seems to have forgotten this passage, we are familiar with it. It is the Bible and not mere tradition that argues that women should be "working at home." What we often miss, however, is Paul's motivation, which demonstrates that this is an issue of the war we are waging: "that the word of God may not be reviled" (Titus

2:5b). Isn't that interesting? When older women fail to teach younger women how to be godly wives and mothers, the Word of God is reviled. The devil scores a victory.

Of course, in another sense, when older women fulfill this command, the Word of God is reviled. That is, those who are in the world, and those who are of the world in the church, hate it. But better to have the seed of the serpent despise the teaching of God's Word than the Seed of the woman.

We need to understand that the Bible looks at the family as a single unit. Each family has a horizontal covenant; all the families together have one vertical covenant with God. We together have been given one job, and that job is to build the kingdom of God. We have one general, one king, and that is the husband. But our daughters are a part of that work, with a central focus on keeping the garden. They should be taught how to be careful stewards of God's provision in their homes. To bring it down to earth a bit more, they need to learn how to bake bread. They need to know how to sew dresses. And to get this done, we need once more to get rid of our baggage.

I have dear friends whom God has blessed with eight children. They homeschooled their children, who were rather typical of homeschoolers. They were delightful. But, as is still too often the case, family and friends would often fuss at them because of the choices they had made. The mother made a confession to me. She told me, "You know, my nine-year-old daughter doesn't know how to read." Now here is a good test to see how much baggage you are carrying around. Does that make you uncomfortable? Are you thinking, "Mercy, what would the school superintendent say if he knew?" My response was a cautious, "Really?" But my friend went on to explain, "She doesn't know how to read, but every morning she gets up and gets ready for the day. Then takes care of her three youngest siblings. She takes them to the potty, she cleans and dresses them, makes their breakfasts, brushes their teeth, clears their dishes, and makes their beds." Now I saw her rightly, as an overachiever. If she didn't know how to read, but did know all the Looney Tunes characters, that would be a problem. But here is a young girl being trained to be a keeper at home. Do I want her to read? Of course I do, as does her mother. I want her to read to equip her to learn the Three Gs. But this little girl was learning what God requires, to be a help in the family business, with a focus on tending the garden.

I'm not suggesting that the goal is to have ignorant daughters. I am, however, arguing that we are to train them to be keepers at home. These two are not equivalent. Though we aren't given many details, we know that both Priscilla and Aquila had a part in the education of Apollos. I'm impressed with Priscilla, as I am with my own wife. She is rather theologically astute. She may come into a conversation I'm having with a student at the Highlands Study Center and zero in on the precise point that needs to be made and make it. Such is a delight to me. I think, "That's my wife! You go, girl." My point is that that brilliance isn't what validates her as a person. It's a good thing, a glorious thing, and an appropriate thing. But it's like the general principle we've already covered. Would I rather be married to a godly woman who was comparatively ignorant, or a wicked person who was terribly bright? Who would make a better wife and mother, someone who doesn't know infra- from supralapsarianism, but does know which side is up on a diaper, or a woman about to defend her dissertation on the eschatology of John Gill at Cambridge but one who thinks children are unpleasant? It's no contest, is it? Naturally, we want everything. We want all the virtues to the highest degree. But virtues come in different shades and colors in different circumstances.

We want to adorn our daughters with virtues that are fitting for them, without making them shrinking violets. There is a sweet little girl with an intriguing name in our church. Her name is Madeline Jael Tremayne. By any standard, "Madeline" is a feminine name, perhaps even a frilly name when associated with the children's books about a little French girl with that name. But right next to Madeline is Jael. Jael isn't a name from a children's story, but from the Bible. Jael is the one who drove a tent peg through the temple of the sleeping Sisera. We want daughters with a gentle and quiet spirit, and daughters with a warrior spirit. And we want both in each of our daughters. We want our daughters to exhibit biblical beauty, as described in 1 Peter: "Do not let your adorning be external—the braiding of hair, the wearing of gold, or the putting on of clothing—but let your adorning be the hidden person of the heart with the imperishable beauty of a gentle and quiet spirit, which in God's sight is very precious" (1 Peter 3:3–4 ESV).

Likewise we must teach our daughters modesty, which involves far more than covering up their bodies. I realized this only recently. I had a child, who for modesty's sake will not be named. This child was struggling with some bad habits. It seemed that the child was always being showy, making silly faces, using silly voices, making silly gestures. I spoke to the child, and told the child, "You need to be more . . ." and then it came to me ". . . modest." "Modest?" the child asked. I explained that all the silliness was an attempt to draw attention, which is immodesty, not a gentle and quiet spirit.

BOYS

There are, of course, specific things that are helpful to <u>boys.</u> One of the tensions that we haven't quite solved yet in homeschooling is the problem of having boys being under men. Too often Daddy is off at some office or factory for the better part of the day. We have moved from <u>working at home to working for home.</u> What a delight, and a help to me, that my work keeps me at home. As I write, my children are up one flight of stairs. That allows for greater occasions when I can interact with my son, not only in terms of ideology, such as when we have our Bible study together, but in terms of manly work as well. Despite my working from an office at home, my wife still does the bulk of what looks like regular school in our household. Apart from being in charge of the R. C. Sproul Jr. School for Spiritual Warfare, I am also in charge of the physical plant.

Recently I was called upon to do an important repair job. The dry-erase board my wife uses had fallen to the ground. The anchors it hung on were secure, but the wire on the back of the board had broken. I had to put a new wire on. There I was, digging around looking for some wire when my son happened into the room. "What are you doing, Daddy?" "I'm getting new wire to hang up the dry erase board." And then I realized I had a teaching opportunity. First, I asked my son to fetch my needle-nose pliers. When he returned with regular pliers, I sent him off with more explicit instructions. I explained to my son that I needed the pliers to cut the wire, and showed him the little circle part at the bottom of the point. I cut one end, and he cut the other.

The truth is that this small job is about the limits of my giftedness. I'm not a terribly handy man. But I want my son first to learn all that I know about such things, before he exceeds me. My son always delights to run errands with me, another opportunity for both of us to learn. When you understand that school is all of life, there is more opportunity for the husband and father to be involved in the homeschool. In fact, we fathers ought not fall into old-fashioned error in reacting against modern feminism. Because the garden is the center of the calling for both husband and wife, we learn that child-rearing isn't just something that women do. It's likewise important for women to remember that they are raising boys, not little copies of themselves. This can be taken too far, when we accept a lack of control as boyishness. But we don't want to raise a nation of sissies either. We don't justify disobedience, a lack of patience, a lack of discipline on the grounds that the child is a boy. But neither do we put the poor child in a skirt. We want boys to grow into an outward-looking, jungle-taming approach to life. (Even when I get to work at home, I still have this outward approach. I'm not advocating that homeschooling fathers become Mr. Mom. I'm advocating that they become Mr. Dad.)

There are likewise different morals that our sons should be taught. All my children are taught these house rules—obey Mommy and Daddy and always speak to Mommy with respect. But my son has an additional rule, one not simply from our house, but one that goes back to the original garden. My son knows: Boys protect girls. Teddy Roosevelt understood that rather well. Long before he was the president, he served, albeit briefly, as a Sunday school teacher. The story is told that a young man came to class with a bloody nose and his clothes in tatters. Mr. Roosevelt asked the young man, in a stern and menacing tone, just what had happened. The boy explained that a bigger boy had been picking on a girl and he lit into him. Teddy gave the boy a dollar, and soon was fired from his job.

I have had my own similar experiences. Once I heard two boys wailing in great pain. I found both boys hard at it. I pulled my son away, asked him what was going on, and he explained that the other boy had been picking on one of his sisters. I told my son I was proud of him. One day my son will be a man. And when that day comes, I want him to feel the weight of responsibility that comes with being a man. (I am careful, by the way, not to put too much of that weight on him now. I never tell him, even in jest when I leave the house, "You take care of the ladies while I'm gone." I can only imagine the trauma he would feel if a real bad guy showed up in my absence and he were unable to resist him.) Boys need to learn to cherish their sisters because a day is coming when they will be called to cherish their wives. That's why even now my son takes the least comfortable seat, why he carries in the heaviest sack of groceries (even though Darby is two years his senior).

On a more practical level, I want my son, very soon, to know how to shoot a gun and clean one. He received a BB gun for his eighth birthday. He thought it was for fun. But I bought it for training. I am more interested in my son's mastering how to shoot and clean a gun than I am his mastering the pantheon of Greek gods.

This is not always easy. Darby's best friend, far and away, is her little brother. Campbell usually isn't terribly excited about playing tea party. Just a few moments ago, on the other hand, I had to break up their sword fight. (Lest you worry, they were using rolled-up magazines for their swords—no actual children were hurt in the making of this point.) Again, I don't want my daughters to be weak. I want them to be Jaels. But I do want them to be women. I want them to submit in the Lord first to their parents and, later, to their own husbands.

In short, we need to be careful not to buy into the unisex nonsense of the world around us. We ought not be ashamed to have a boy curriculum and a girl curriculum, because we are raising boys and girls. Or better still, we are raising men and women. Our goal is to raise godly seed, which in turn means raising godly men and godly women. The neighbors or the in-laws won't understand, but that will be just one more blessing that comes from obedience. Your children might not exactly fit in with the other children on the block, but that is precisely the point. Your children will thank you, and better still, your grandchildren will thank you. May they all have an ever-increasing zeal for the Lord's kingdom, and an ever-increasing obedience to his Word.

OBJECTIONS ANSWERED

6

We live in an age of sophistry. The ancient Greeks ran head-on into the problem of the one and the many. Long before Socrates roamed the land, Parmenides made it into the history books by siding with the one when he opined, "Whatever is, is." His ideological opponent, Heraclitus, had a different perspective. Fighting on the side of the many, he affirmed, "Whatever is, is changing." One saw a static universe, the other an unintelligible cacophony. As they and their students sought in vain a synthesis (which, by the way, can be found only in affirming both the one and the many, or to put it more clearly, the one and the three), a new group of "philosophers" emerged. Despairing over any resolution, these fellows took a more pragmatic approach. They determined not only that the problem of the one and the many would not be solved, but that we can't really know anything anyway. The function of philosophy wasn't so much to discern the higher truths as it was to learn the art of persuasion. To the sophist, all language was simply a power grab, and the wise used that power for their own selfish ends. (Sound familiar?) The trouble is, the sophists then and now can get so sophisticated that they end up fooling themselves.

Here is how sophistry might work in my house. Suppose my wife says, "Tomorrow night we're going to have chicken tahini on a bed of fresh pasta with grated Asiago cheese." Suppose in turn that I reply, "Wow, dear, that sounds wonderful. But boneless chicken doesn't grow on trees. Fresh pasta is rather more expensive than the dry kind, and do you know how much tahini costs, or Asiago cheese?" This might be a perfectly sound argument. My wife might even buy it. I am, after all, a rather tight fellow. But she might also know me well enough that while I am somewhat cheap, the one place I'm most apt to splurge on is what I put in my belly. As a sophist I'm not interested in the truth. My real objection, that I don't like chicken tahini, isn't the point. The goal is to persuade my wife. If I tell her the truth, she might get her back up. She might think I'm saying I don't like her cooking. But if I appeal to the checkbook, she might ally herself with me on the question. And maybe, in the end, we'll get to have what I like, something good and cheap— grilled-cheese sandwiches.

We all face the temptation to raise objections we think will stick rather than our true objections, but we might even do this unknowingly. Often someone obviously upset approaches me after I have spoken at a conference. He or she begins with objection A to what I have spoken about. We open our Bibles together, and find that objection A has no merit. In the bat of an eyelash, we're on to objection B. We deal with that, and we're off to objection C until I begin to suspect that the real problem is objection R. C.—that the person doesn't have any objections to anything I've said, just to me.

In the context of homeschooling, I have found that objections come mostly from those who have never tried homeschooling. However, sometimes families homeschool for a time, and then stop. I am surprised that this happens at all, and I am shocked at how often it happens. Last year I was invited to address a local group of homeschoolers in the next state over. That isn't terribly unusual. What was unusual was the response when I asked my hostess what she would like me to speak on while I was there. She said, "Well, we are losing so many of them so quickly—we wanted you to encourage them to stay the course. Can you do that?" Why would anyone stop homeschooling?

I'm convinced that it is not because of a rational, coherent argument. I'm convinced of that both deductively and inductively. That is, it can't be a rational, coherent argument against homeschooling because there is no rational, coherent argument against homeschooling. And secondly, I've spoken with ex-homeschoolers, and they've never even tried to offer an argument. I've never met ex-homeschooling parents who said, "Yes, we've done this for six or seven years, but then someone asked me, 'What about x?' and I didn't have an answer, so

I quit." We don't lose arguments. Instead we get worn out, tired, and seduced. We get weary, and sometimes we're not even sure what it is we've grown weary of.

That's why it is so important to think through these issues in a careful, unemotional way. As I'm writing this book, I am torn between my roles as an evangelist and as an encourager. I pray that countless thousands of families will read this book, bring their children home, and teach them the Three Gs through a life of conversation. I pray also that thousands of homeschooling families will stop doing school-at-home, and start teaching their children the Three Gs through a life of conversation. But, if nothing else, I pray that this book will serve as a hedge against parents who are tempted to go back to Egypt, who are longing for leeks and garlic.

I want all of us to be clear on why we are doing these things. If you are already a committed homeschooler, if you have found what you have read to be biblical, I want you to be able to exhort others along the same path. In your conversations with friends, family, and neighbors, I want you to be equipped to exhort others to walk the right path. It's much like evangelism. I don't want to hear from you, asking me to come close the deal: "I met this person and we got on the subject of homeschooling and ... and ... would you mind coming to meet with them, R. C.?" We not only need to understand why we do what we do, but also need to understand the objections of those who do not do what we do, both the spoken objections and the unspoken.

I'm convinced that the number-one objection to homeschooling is the one that is never spoken out loud. I believe the reason people begin rejecting homeschooling is that they are convinced that it is too big a responsibility. Of course, this is something of a guess, because the objection is unspoken. It may, in fact, be me projecting my own fears. Or I may be on to something. My dear wife and I, as I write, are busy right now raising six blessings. Given our ages, and given how God has acted in the past in our own lives, without anything too terribly unusual happening, we could have ten blessings to raise.

When I think about raising ten children, what do you think I worry about? Do you think I worry how I could possibly afford to care for ten children? Not in the slightest. That is the least of my worries. From an earthly perspective, I live in the most prosperous nation in history, at the most prosperous time in history. Feeding, clothing, and sheltering ten children isn't too terribly expensive an ordeal. Now, it certainly would be a challenge if I were to do this while keeping up with the Joneses. But that's not the goal. And from a heavenly perspective, "I have been young, and now am old; yet I have not seen the righteous forsaken, nor his descendants begging bread" (Ps. 37:25). The same God who has blessed me with six, and who could bless me with more, is the God to whom I pray with confidence, "Give us this day our daily bread. . . ." No, money is not my concern.

Am I worried about giving enough attention to ten children? No, I'm not worried about that. In God's economy, with each additional child he gives, there is a corresponding increase in the number of people able to give attention. That is, each child would have not only two parents, but nine siblings. We believe that children are a blessing for the believer. We delight in all that God will send.

But with each child I do feel a burden of responsibility. It is a real weight. God not only gives us the children, but also calls us to raise them in the nurture and admonition of the Lord. That's a scary business. If I were to buy myself a sailboat, I would also have a responsibility to keep it in shape— I would need to polish the brass, tend to the sails, keep track of the life vests, and mend leaks. If I failed in my duty, the worst that could happen is that my boat would fall apart or sink. No great loss—it's only a boat! Instead, I have these little children to nurture. Unlike a sailboat, children last forever, either in eternal joy or, eternal anguish. It is scary business.

But how foolish to try to deal with that fear by putting our heads in the sand. We're like little babies playing peek-a-boo. Scientists tell us that when little children cover their eyes and can't see you, they jump to the conclusion that you can't see them. We think if we ignore the weight of this calling that it isn't there. You can recognize the weight of training your children, of raising them in the nurture and admonition of the Lord. It is indeed a great responsibility. You can't, however, change your mind and decide not to so raise your children because it's too hard. They are your responsibility, and denying your responsibility won't change your situation.

Of course, this objection escapes our lips in different forms. No one says, "I'm afraid of responsibility." What we hear too often instead is, "I'm not a good teacher. I can't home-school." But there is a fallacious unspoken premise here. The argument is really, "I'm not a good teacher. I shouldn't have to do anything I'm not good at. Therefore I won't be a teacher." But what would we say to a parent if, having brought to their attention that their children are running about like hurricanes destroying everything in their path, they were to explain, "Oh, I'm not a very good disciplinarian." Or suppose at the end of the month the boss comes around and says, "We're getting ready to write out checks for employees this month, but we've noticed that we haven't gotten any output from you." Would it make sense for you to explain, "Well, you see, I'm not a very good worker"?

I had a dear friend in college who never seemed to get this. He tended to get into various kinds of trouble. He did foolish things. He was rather insecure, and allowed himself to be jerked around by other people. When he'd be in some kind of mess, and I would go to him to gently chasten him for his foolishness, before I could even start he would say, "I know, I know. I'm a big fat jerk." It was as if he thought, "Now you cannot correct me; you cannot chasten me. All you can do is walk away, because it's already been said." Despite the talk of pop-psychologists, admitting a failure is _not_ half the battle. You have to solve the problem. The answer to the objection "But I'm not a good teacher" is "Become a good teacher." The answer to "But I'm no good at disciplining the children" is "Discipline your-self to be good at disciplining the children." The answer to "My children don't respect me" is "And they never will as long as you send them off to some school to have someone else raise them." If God calls you to do something, you do it. You don't whine about it, delegate it, or pretend you didn't hear him and hope he'll go away. If we have understood Deuteronomy 6 properly, then he has called parents to be the teachers of their children. How good we are at it is beside the point.

This same objection takes a slight twist, however, when it comes from the outside. No doubt some parents believe they aren't good teachers because some outsider has already told them, "You aren't qualified." This objection finds a foothold only because we yet hold on to the world's goals. What are we aiming for? When someone says, "You're not qualified," ask him or her this: "Not qualified for what?" There are, after all, many things I'm not qualified to do. In fact, there are many things I'm not qualified to do that the state schools are highly qualified to do. I'm thinking of at least one job for which I may be the least qualified person in the world. If we could give an aptitude test for this skill, I believe I would fall in dead last. Everyone else on the entire planet, I believe, is better equipped than I am to raise a servant of the state. I'm not the guy to do that job. I am, however, equipped to raise servants of the King. I know that because the King keeps giving me servants to raise.

What does it take to raise children in the nurture and admonition of the Lord? The Bible, and the Holy Spirit to illumine the Bible. I have a Bible. I have several, in fact. And the Bible tells me that it equips me for every good work. It is a good work to raise my children in the nurture and admonition of the Lord. Therefore, it equips me to raise children in the nurture and admonition of the Lord. Let's remember our biblical wisdom here. Too often we answer the fool according to his folly. When the qualification argument is made, too many of us reach for our diplomas. Our answer ought not to be, "Well, the really smart people down at State U. tell me that I'm a reasonably smart person, so I'm qualified." All that really tells you, however, is that you probably have a great deal of "wisdom" to unlearn.

We need to be careful of the same line of reasoning on the other end. A year or so ago a well-respected Christian radio teacher did several of his shows on the subject of homeschooling. On the face of it, that's a good thing. I was delighted to hear this influential man speak to Christians so favorably about homeschooling. On the show I happened to hear, however, he had a pair of brothers as guests. These boys were in their early teens, and had been homeschooled all their lives. These two kids were classic high achievers. One of them was the state champion in his age group in golf. Both played first chair in the state youth orchestra. The older one had even played his violin at one of President Bush's inaugural balls. Both of them were county chess champions in their age brackets. Each brother had his own business. One designed web pages; the other was a motivational speaker (at 12, he hoped to become the next Zig Ziglar). These young men had accomplished great things. I'm delighted at their success. But the message on that program that day was, "Your kids can be better than their kids, by their standards." But we don't live by their standards.

A dear friend had heard the program, and missed the point. He was a godly man, and was so excited about what he had heard. After reciting what these young men had done, his ecstatic conclusion was, "These homeschool kids can go and get into Harvard." He was so excited you would have thought Jesus was coming back tomorrow. I had to explain, "You're not getting it! Getting into Harvard isn't the goal, for two reasons. The students at Harvard aren't so bright by biblical standards, and we're more interested in raising godly children than smart children."

One way we help people see the folly of the demand for qualifications and the need for an expert is by way of analogy. Did you know, for instance, that there are children in these United States who are being fed by unqualified feeders? Many of these unqualified feeders haven't finished a college degree, and even of those who have, precious few of them have degrees in feeding. These people haven't bothered to get a feeding license from the state. That's the truly scary part—there is no way for oversight over these unlicensed feeders. They don't bring their children to the public feeding places. This, by the way, hurts the feeding scores of the other children left at the public feeding places, and takes public funds away from the feeding places. That's why the private feeding must stop. Friends, why is the absurdity of the above easy to see, but when we replace feeding with teaching it suddenly looks so sane?

Of course, there are circumstances in which qualifications make sense. I'm not so egalitarian or so down on expertise that if I had clogged arteries I would let you have at my heart with the toy angioplasty kit you keep in your car. I want my heart surgeon to be an expert. I want the elders in the church to meet the biblical qualifications of an elder. But what are the qualifications necessary to be a teacher? Having a child. God gives you a child and says, "You teach him. By my grace, through my power, with my Holy Spirit, you teach him." The answer to the qualification objection is this—God gave me this child.

There is yet another, gentler objection to homeschooling, especially prevalent from our friends in the classical-school movement. Here it is called the "efficiency" argument. Isn't it more efficient, these folks argue, for one person to teach twenty-five small children phonics, grammar, and Latin than to have twenty-five overwhelmed moms (each with older and younger children) try to teach their own? If someone else can do the job more efficiently than I can, isn't that better? Isn't everyone in favor of higher efficiency? Suppose, for a moment, that it *were* more efficient to send your children off to a classical Christian school. Is efficiency the highest good? God not only commands us to teach our children the Three Gs, but also commands us to fill the earth. Is lifelong monogamy really the most efficient way to fulfill that goal? Couldn't we fill the earth faster with the practice of "free love"?

But that would be sin. That would be against God's law. In short, God not only gives the command, the end result he wants, but also gives the how-to, the way he wants that result met. God didn't say to parents, "Find the most efficient way to make sure your children know the Three Gs and get to it."

Instead he called parents to do the job. What if it actually were more efficient for us to gather our six-year-olds in one room, our seven-year-olds in another, and our eight-year-olds in a third? Or have our ten-, eleven-, twelve-, and thirteen-year-olds move from room to room to have the efficient Greek expert in one room, the efficient Latin expert in another, and the efficient rhetoric expert in the third? If God tells parents to teach their children, doesn't that settle the question?

Please understand that I'm not actually conceding anything on the efficiency question. I'm just saying even if the school model is superior by that standard, it fails the Bible's standard. If we really want efficiency in raising our children in the nurture and admonition of the Lord, then we need to ask some important questions. Who knows your child better, you or the recent Christian college graduate at the local classical school? Who has the greater vested interest in raising your child in the nurture and admonition of the Lord, you or that same young lady with the education degree? Now we have these questions: How long is the commute to your homeschool compared to the commute to the "local" classical school? How much gas do you burn getting to the school? How much insurance do you pay for that commute? Which is more efficient, for you to go out and get a job to earn the money to pay someone to do the job, or for you to do the job?

If God were to bless my dear wife and me with ten children, which ratio would be more efficient, one to ten, or one to twenty or thirty? I concede that the twenty or thirty might all be the same age. But the ten, on the other hand, are all

Sprouls. When there are ten of them, and the youngest is finally ready for more formal schooling, the ratio isn't really one to ten. It's more like four to six, which is more efficient. How many teacher's aides does a family of ten have? Rather a few.

I suppose it is possible to also hear this objection: "We can't afford it." Every summer, when my dear Denise is spending her evenings with garters on her sleeves and a green-tinted visor on her head, when I see her with a pen in her mouth, a calculator on her desk, and a clutch of homeschool catalogues in her talons, I am reminded that homeschooling is not free. But the "I can't afford it" argument, nine times out of ten (with the possible exception of parents who are teachers at classical and Christian schools), is an argument for state schools. Homeschooling may not be free, but it's much less expensive than a Christian school. Either way, however, it is no argument, and is built on faulty premises. The quick answer is, "Can you afford a Bible?" This is where the rubber meets the road. It certainly may be expensive to buy video classes from Acme Homeschool-in-a-Box Company. It may be expensive to buy new gold-leaf copies of everything you'll need for the "Well-Trained Mind Classical School in Your Home" curriculum series. If the content of your children's education is to be the Bible, then that's all it need cost. If finances are tight, it may be that your children won't get to learn the entire Roman and Greek pantheons. Or at least they won't get to learn them using the latest full-color flashcards from Highbrow Press.

Now, I'm not suggesting that it is always a bad thing to have a class on video, or that we should never read Thucydides.

I'm against neither Roman gods nor flashcards. I'm also not against cars made by Lexus. But I am against anyone's arguing that they have to have a government car because they can't afford a Lexus. It just doesn't follow.

There is yet another line of argument, this one having a slightly more pious tint to it. The various forms of this argument all come under the heading I like to call "the well-being of the child" argument: "I can't teach my child x, and in today's fast paced economy, everybody has to know x." Once again we need to go back to the standard. Can you teach your children the Bible? If the answer is yes, you are ready to homeschool. If the answer is no, then you must devote every moment you have to becoming trained to teach your children the Bible, because somehow God, in his mysterious providence, has given you a child and not equipped you for every good work. So learn the Bible. If you can't teach them physics, then you can't teach them physics. If you can't teach them geography, then you can't teach them geography. If you are able, and you want to teach those things, then do so. But if you don't know the Bible, learn the Bible.

The most pathetic version of "the well-being of the child" is, more often than not, more like "the faded glory of the parent." That is, some parents actually decide on how to educate their children based on the best available sports programs. Once again it is important not to answer a fool according to his folly here, pointing out the athletic success of this homeschooler or that one. Nor do we swiftly steer the conversation to sports opportunities outside the local school. Those things may be perfectly okay, in moderation. They ought never to be used to trump the Bible. If Deuteronomy 6 teaches that parents are to teach their children, then your family's lack of a varsity football team matters none.

One of the most compelling arguments I've ever heard *for* homeschooling is this one given against it: "My child will rebel if I homeschool him." The solution for parents who have lost control is never to give up more control. That our children identify more with a circle of friends, a peer group, than they do with our family is the problem, not the solution. If your daughter is more committed to this alternative family of her friends down at the mall, she needs to be removed from that family, and brought back into the repentant family that allowed things to get this far. The same reasoning applies, by the way, for the variant of this argument: "I agree with everything you've said. I see what the Bible teaches. But it's too late for me." Is it ever too late to obey? Of course, my prayer is that every family would homeschool from birth. If that's not you, my prayer is that you will homeschool from now on. It may require difficult changes. It may require the awkward work of repenting to your wife and to your children for how you have abdicated your responsibility. Get used to it. Even those of us who have homeschooled from birth find ourselves repenting to our wives and children with regularity. That there is a need to repent is a sign that all is not right. When we actually do repent, however, that's a positive, a good thing.

The well-being of the child can include any number of silly things, depending on what extracurricular activity the parent has the fondest memories of. "Why, if I homeschool the children, how will they ever get to work on the yearbook ... go to the prom ... be the homecoming queen ... go to college?" Each of these is an appeal to pragmatism. There are, of course, homeschoolers who will answer each of these fools according to their follies. There are homeschool sports teams, cheerleading squads, proms, yearbooks, field trips, and bake sales to pay for all this stuff.

Certainly homeschoolers go to college. But we are living in a culture that is increasingly hostile to the Christian faith, and for a time, anyway, that is going to require some adjustment. Roughly twenty years ago, the American Medical Association, the physicians union that has the authority to license doctors and medical schools, nearly required all medical-school programs to include a rotation in abortion. Had they succeeded, from that point forward, anyone wanting to be a medical doctor would have been required to perform an abortion as part of his or her training. Had the AMA succeeded, I trust we would have seen no more young Christians entering the medical profession. For a field to have certain requirements doesn't change the law of God. Abandoning that field for a time, in obedience to the law, may be the only choice.

There are but two objections left that I am aware of, one from the left, and one from the right. The one from the left is the granddaddy of them all: "What about socialization?" Before we begin to look at the question, let's consider once again what the Bible tells us. It tells us that it equips us for every good work. It tells us likewise that we are to raise our children in the nurture and admonition of the Lord. But it not only doesn't tell us how to socialize our children, but doesn't tell us that they should be socialized. There is no commandment from God, "Thou shalt socialize thy children." In fact, I'm sometimes a little unclear as to what it is these objectors are seeking for my children. What does it mean to be socialized?

Sometimes I ask those who raise this objection, "Now, when you speak of socialization, you're talking about my child's ability to get along with others who are different. Is that it?" Usually I get some sort of affirmative response. "I see," I go on, "and your solution is for my ten-year-old to spend seven hours a day stuck in a room with a bunch of other ten-year-olds?" My daughter Darby interacts with different kinds of people far more than any child at a state school. She interacts every day with her mommy and daddy. I'm not like a ten-year-old girl at all. She spends hours on end with her eight-year-old brother Campbell. She "socializes" with her sister Delaney (five). She reads to her sister Erin Claire (three), and she often gets her sister Maili (one) out of her crib in the morning. Not only that, but for the past six years Darby has been part of a mainstreaming program during the school year and during nonschool days. She interacts with her special-needs little sister Shannon.

She does have friends from church, not because we schedule "socialization" time for her, but because our family is friends with all the families in the church. She interacts with the therapists who come to help Shannon every week. She interacts with the folks at the grocery store, at the post office, and at the Highlands Study Center. She visits with and serves visiting missionaries and their families. Next month she will be interacting with Korean Christians as she travels with her dad to Seoul, where he will be teaching at a seminary and speaking at a homeschool conference.

But this isn't really what people mean by socialization. What they want for my daughter Darby is for her to be hip to all the things other ten-year-old girls are concerned about, like fashion labels, television shows, pop singers, and other essentials to the good life. They are concerned that my daughter is not under the sway of Madison Avenue, that she is free. But I have none of that concern. I raise my daughter, her sisters, and her brother to be free. Their identity is in Christ, not in pop culture.

Oh, but how will she ever meet people where they are? How will she ever be able to relate to the world around her, if she doesn't know what's up with Harry Potter? And if she doesn't know that, how can she possibly win the lost? This whole drowning-ourselves-in-pop-culture-sludge argument should be wearing rather thin by now. What exactly do your children need to know in order to win the lost besides the Bible, the very center of our curriculum? Everyone remembers the encounter between Philip and the Ethiopian eunuch. Does Philip approach the eunuch and ask, "So, how is the Ethiopian bobsledding team doing this year? I was up late last night trying to get a report on ESPN, but I must have fallen asleep. Mercy, I'm still tired. Do you mind if I take a nap here in your cart? Maybe when I wake up I'll tell you about Jesus."

All our children need to know about the lost is that they are lost. When they, in their lostness, yammer on and on about the latest boy band, all they need to know is that the latest boy band isn't the answer.

Now to our final objection that comes from within the Christian church. Here the concern isn't that if we homeschool our children, they won't be hip enough to win the lost, but that if we homeschool, they won't ever run into the lost. That is, when we homeschool we fail to send our children out into a dying world as salt and as light. After all, isn't the purpose of education that our children might have an opportunity to serve as missionaries? Of all the objections we've considered, this one at least has the virtue of not being motivated by the same greedy pursuit of personal peace and affluence that drives the world. I don't doubt that there are parents who sincerely believe it their duty to send their children into a hostile environment for the sake of the lost. Their sincerity, however, doesn't make them right.

There are two things, on the other hand, that cause me to question that sincerity. First, there is always a line drawn. I've never met a parent who determined to send their teenage child off to a brothel or a crack house for the sake of the lost. The people there are as lost as the people at the state school. The only difference is, in the brothel or the crack house, the bad guys don't have the authority to make our children sit and listen to their worldview being taught for seven hours a day. But there's another cause for my doubts. I have yet to hear of a parent who is so concerned for the lost that they actually pay to send their children to attend a Muslim school, or a Roman Catholic school. Isn't it at least suspicious that all those who are motivated to send their children out as missionaries send them where it is "free" to attend?

Do I care about the lost? Of course I do. Do my children care about the lost? Enough that they can pray for them at school, out loud, every day. I am homeschooling precisely so my children will be able to know, recognize, and love the enemy, while not becoming the enemy. And just as their ability to love the enemy into the kingdom isn't contingent on their being trained by the enemy, in like manner their ability to love the enemy into the kingdom isn't contingent on their being in the enemy's schools. The greatest thing our children can do for the lost is to so let their light shine before men that they glorify their Father in heaven. My children do, by the grace of God, show forth the glory of the gospel. They humble their father, by constantly eliciting the praise of men for their good behavior. I don't want their bushels buried. But neither do I want their flames extinguished. Never will I put my children under the authority of those who are enemies of the gospel, who despise the lordship of Christ such that his name cannot even be mentioned. That we must never negotiate.

And therein is the end of the matter. I have tried to make the case in this book, under the authority of Christ, that parents are commanded to train up their children in the nurture and admonition of the Lord. But let me concede this. While biblical education is done by parents' teaching the Three Gs to their children when they rise up and when they lie down, the most grievous error we can make is to send them off to schools where Jesus is not plainly, fully, and publicly honored. In that great name may we hasten the day when no parent at the same time claims to serve the King, and yet allows his child to be trained by those who will not name that King. May it never be said again of any of those who name the name of Christ that they rendered unto Caesar the things that are God's—his covenant children.

A CONCLUDING UNSCIENTIFIC POSTSCRIPT

It can't be that simple, can it? As I set about the task of persuading you first to homeschool and second to do it by speaking with your children about the Three Gs, one of the rhetorical strikes against me is how simple it is. Because we are children of the Enlightenment, we are more impressed with lengthy expositions of complex theories. But as the children of the living God, we are called to the faith of children. So if your response is, "It can't be that simple, can it?" my last word is, "Yes, it actually is."

You have slogged through a book-length treatment of an incredibly ancient and simple truth—that we teach our children by talking with them of the things of God. This truth is so hoary that by comparison the classical model still hasn't sprouted any peach fuzz. This truth is not the Puritan model, not the Reformers' program, not the method that brought us da Vinci or Aquinas or Augustine. It's what God told Moses to tell his children to do.

What we don't need is a movement. We don't need associations and agencies, press releases and pedagogues, development officers and dialogical facilitators. We don't need parents who look earnestly off into some bright future, while dutifully laying groundwork in the here and now to build the bridge to tomorrow. Instead we need faithful parents who will look earnestly into their children's eyes, smile honestly, and tell them about the glory of God. We don't even need dreamers wondering how the world might look different if parents spoke of these things to their children when they lie down and when they rise up. What we need are curious parents who instead wonder how their children might look different if they spoke with them of these things when they lie down and when they rise up. By the grace of God, may we have the wisdom to act in faith, and to dream small.

R. C. Sproul Jr. (M.A., Reformed Theological Seminary, Orlando; D.Min., Whitefield Theological Seminary) is a pastor at St. Peter Presbyterian Church, Bristol, Tennessee, and director of the Highlands Study Center, Meadowview, Virginia. He is also editor-in-chief of *Every Thought Captive*. Sproul has authored several books including *Tearing Down Strongholds, Almighty over All, Playing God,* and *Eternity in Our Hearts*. He also writes a regular column for *Homeschooling Today* magazine. R. C. and his wife, Denise, have six children.